T0293495

THE POWER OF HOPE

The Power of Hope

How the Science
of Well-Being
Can Save Us
from Despair

Carol Graham

PRINCETON UNIVERSITY PRESS
PRINCETON AND OXFORD

Published by Princeton University Press
41 William Street, Princeton, New Jersey 08540
99 Banbury Road, Oxford OX2 6JX

press.princeton.edu

All Rights Reserved

Library of Congress Cataloging-in-Publication Data

Names: Graham, Carol, 1962– author.
Title: The power of hope : how the science of well-being
    can save us from despair / Carol Graham.
Description: 1st. | Princeton : Princeton University Press,
    [2023] | Includes bibliographical references and index.
Identifiers: LCCN 2022036335 (print) | LCCN 2022036336 (ebook) | ISBN
    9780691233437 (hardback ; alk. paper) | ISBN 9780691233901 (ebook)
Subjects: LCSH: Economics—Psychological aspects. | Hope—
    Psychological aspects. | Hope—Economic aspects. | Quality
    of life. | Well-being. | BISAC: BUSINESS & ECONOMICS /
    Economic Conditions | PSYCHOLOGY / Social Psychology
Classification: LCC HB74.P8 G732 2023 (print) | LCC HB74.
    P8 (ebook) | DDC 330.01/9—dc23/eng/20220728
LC record available at https://lccn.loc.gov/2022036335
LC ebook record available at https://lccn.loc.gov/2022036336

British Library Cataloging-in-Publication Data is available

Editorial: Joe Jackson, Josh Drake, and Whitney Rauenhorst
Production Editorial: Natalie Baan
Production: Erin Suydam
Publicity: Kate Farquhar-Thomson, Kate Hensley, and James Schneider
Copyeditor: Leah Caldwell

This book has been composed in Source Serif 4 and Gotham

Printed on acid-free paper. ∞

Printed in the United States of America

10 9 8 7 6 5 4 3 2 1

To Alexander, Anna, and Adrian,
who are not only the roots of my own hopes
but are also helping those hopes come alive
as they each, in their own way, try to make
the world a better place.

CONTENTS

This book is a result of my experience from two decades of involvement with well-being research in economics and in policy. At the same time, this book is a reflection of my concerns about the stark challenges of ill-being facing the United States, one of the wealthiest but also one of the most divided countries in the world. For the two decades that I have been active in contributing to the increasingly robust and promising "science" of well-being, with a particular focus on what it can contribute to economics and to public policy, I have also been aware of the divisions in the United States growing markedly. These divisions are between the rich and the poor, across racial groups, between political parties, and between different sectors of civil society.

I was puzzled for a long time by the lack of public and political attention to these divisions and to their manifestation in the growing gaps in opportunities across racial and socioeconomic lines. My recent research and last book, *Happiness for All? Unequal Hopes and Lives in Pursuit of the American Dream*, explored how these divisions were reflected in differences in well-being in our society and how they manifested in very different levels of hope—and despair. It seemed intuitive to me that people would resonate more with learning that hope was unequally shared than by hearing that the Gini coefficient had increased to .437 (even though that number reflects that the United States—the so-called land of opportunity—is entering the ranks of the most unequal countries in the world).[1]

---

1 This is based on Congressional Budget Office after-tax figures for 2018, the latest estimate, increasing from 0.352 in 1979; the pretax number is much higher. I thank Gary Burtless for clarifying the pretax and posttax distinctions.

My initial explorations yielded, not surprisingly, high levels of inequality across the rich and the poor in many different well-being markers, ranging from life satisfaction to stress to belief that hard work can get individuals ahead. More important and more surprisingly, the marker that stood out the most was not in happiness but rather in hope for the future. And it stood out not only for the large differences across the rich and the poor (greater than in Latin America), but also for very large differences across races, with African Americans being by far the most optimistic racial group and low-income African Americans having the largest gaps with other low-income counterparts, particularly white ones (something that I have been working on since then with my wonderful coauthor, Sergio Pinto).

I found these patterns in mid-2015—before we even knew of the crisis of deaths of despair. When the first study documenting those deaths by Anne Case and Angus Deaton (2015) came out later that year, I realized that the patterns I was uncovering in well-being matched those in actual mortality rates and that well-being metrics could be useful tracking tools and even preventive ones. I also delved, with Kelsey O'Connor (2019), into historical trends in optimism and found that despair began to increase among less-than-college-educated white men in the late 1970s, at the time of the first major decline in manufacturing, while trends in optimism were increasing among women and African Americans, as gender rights and civil rights improved.

Since then, I have focused on what we can learn from the increasingly extensive well-being research on combating despair and on creating mechanisms whereby well-being metrics can serve as tracking tools. The more I have been involved in that effort, with many wonderful colleagues whom I acknowledge throughout the book, all roads point to the seemingly elusive goal of restoring hope in populations where it has been lost. Perhaps like Don Quixote tilting at

windmills, in this book I aim to convince unlikely types—
academic economists, policymakers, and epidemiologists,
among others—that hope is relevant to so many kinds of outcomes, to the extent that we should measure it routinely in
our statistics and include it in our research efforts.

I surely have not convinced all or even many of the skep-
tics, but there are signs of progress. Some signs of progress
are in other countries, such as the United Kingdom, which
has routinely included well-being metrics in its national statistics since 2012 and most recently has made reducing well-
being inequalities the framing objective for its Levelling Up
initiative. New Zealand, meanwhile, now uses well-being as
a frame for setting its budgetary and policy priorities. Some
signs of progress are also reflected in the work of our key foundations, such as the Robert Wood Johnson Foundation, the
largest funder of health research in the United States, which
now routinely includes funding for research on well-being
and, specifically, hope (including my own, for full disclosure).
The National Endowment for the Arts, meanwhile, is funding research that explores the potential of the arts to restore
community hope and well-being. Some progress is also reflected in the dedicated efforts of local practitioners around
the country who are involved in day-to-day efforts to revive
hope in desperate and declining communities. I have learned
a great deal and take pride in knowing many of the people
involved in those efforts.

Equally important, I am driven by my personal belief—and
perhaps stubbornness—that we cannot let hope—along with
faith in democratic institutions— fade in the world's oldest
democracy. I was born in Peru and grew up between Peru
and the United States, learning early on (largely through the
work of my father and the talented team at the Instituto de
Investigación Nutricional—an institute that he founded, focused on the challenges of childhood malnutrition) about the
long reach that extreme poverty can have on people's lives. At

the same time, I also experienced the remarkable resiliency that many poor individuals display in the face of daunting challenges. For the first several decades of my life, traveling between the two countries, including at a time when Peru was plagued by hyperinflation and Shining Path terrorism, I thought of the United States as a beacon of democracy and stable institutions.

Yet for the past two decades, I have wondered why there is so much despair—and mistrust of institutions—in one of the wealthiest countries in the world, and why the poor of Latin America retain their hope and resilience in the face of constant challenges. We now even face a threat from right-wing terrorism from within. There is also the question of why there is more hope among poor minorities—who have traditionally faced discrimination and injustice—than among poor whites. I cannot say I have all the answers, but I think I have some, as well as some lessons about hope and resilience that I believe are transferrable across borders and populations. I also am increasingly convinced, not least because of the challenges that the COVID-19 pandemic has posed to mental health and well-being worldwide, that the time has come to reorient our objectives for public policy from economic progress alone to societal well-being. We now have a robust measurement science and sufficient policy experience to do so.

This book is a summary of what we know from empirical research on hope and well-being; it is also a warning about the urgency of the moment. I am not only concerned about despair among today's populations, I am concerned about despair among future generations, among those who will neither be able to pursue gainful and purposeful employment nor look forward to better futures for themselves and their children. The current crisis threatens our health and well-being, our democracy, our civil society, and even our national security. Lost hope is an integral part of the equation. We must find a solution.

ACKNOWLEDGMENTS

I could, of course, not have even envisioned this without the help and inspiration of many colleagues, mentors, and friends. It is, without a doubt, a risky enterprise for an economist to write a treatise on hope, and then an entire book, with just a little empirical econometric analysis that asserts the topic is important and that the key variable can cause good things. I have done just that. I could not have done it without confidence inspired by the giants I followed in the footsteps of. These include George Akerlof, Richard Easterlin, Danny Kahneman, Richard Layard, Gus O'Donnell, and Andrew Oswald, among others. I also could not have done it without the hardheaded (but not hardhearted) critique of other giants, such as Henry Aaron, Alan Angell, Gary Burtless, Angus Deaton, Steven Durlauf (who was very helpful with the research on adolescent aspirations), Belle Sawhill, Peyton Young, and the late Alice Rivlin.

I also both benefited and learned from so many wonderful colleagues, such as Dany Bahar, Danny Blanchflower, Mary Blankenship, Anita Chandra, Soumya Chattopadhyay, Andrew Clark, Kemal Dervis, Emily Dobson, Jan Emmanuel de Neve, Harris Eyre, Michal Grinstein-Weiss, Ross Hammond, Nancy Hey, Fiona Hill, Homi Kharas, Edward Lawlor, Kelsey O'Connor, Sergio Pinto, Nick Powdthavee, Jonathan Rauch, Richard Reeves, and Julie Rusk. I also had wonderful research assistance from—and lots of fun working with—James Kuhnhardt, Tim Hua, Ani Bannerjee, and Andrew Zarhan. I also have to thank a number of Brookings colleagues, including David Batcheck, Merrell Tuck-Prindahl, Brahima Coulibay, Esther Rosen, and Sebastian Strauss.

I also had wonderful support—both financial and intellectual—from Karobi Acharya, Alonso Plough, and Paul Tarini at the Robert Wood Johnson Foundation; Ben Miller of Wellbeing Trust; Andy Keller of the Meadows Mental Health Institute; and Sunil Iyengar of the National Endowment for the Arts. Two successive and wonderful Brookings' presidents—Strobe Talbott and John Allen—have provided me with the resources and confidence to pursue research that was initially considered crazy but now is considered essential, at least by some. I am grateful to them all.

I also thank the wonderful team at Princeton University Press, especially Joe Jackson, Josh Drake, James Schneider, Natalie Baan, and Leah Caldwell. I am also grateful for the helpful comments of two reviewers.

Finally, I am thankful for the support and patience of my three wonderful children, Alexander, Anna, and Adrian, who understand me trying to make the world a better place—even though it is hard to succeed—and now have begun to pursue their own dreams. One is a dedicated journalist at a time when it is so much needed yet the rewards make it difficult to make ends meet; one is going into medical school debt to pursue her passion in public health; and one is becoming a CPA, so that he can help finance the rest of our dreams! I am so proud of them and so grateful for the hope they give me for the next generation. They embody why hope matters.

THE POWER OF HOPE

CHAPTER 1

Introduction

Our mission is to plant ourselves at the gates of Hope—not the prudent gates of Optimism, which are somewhat narrower; nor the stalwart, boring gates of Common Sense; nor the strident gates of Self-Righteousness, which creak on shrill and angry hinges (people cannot hear us there; they cannot pass through); nor the cheerful, flimsy garden gate of "Everything is gonna be all right." But a different, sometimes lonely place, the place of truth-telling, about your own soul first of all and its condition, the place of resistance and defiance, the piece of ground from which you see the world both as it is and as it could be, as it will be; the place from which you glimpse not only struggle, but joy in the struggle. And we stand there, beckoning and calling, telling people what we are seeing, asking people what they see.

—**Victoria Safford**[1]

Hope is a little studied concept in economics. Yet it matters. It is, as the poem above notes, more open-ended than optimism focused on the foreseeable future. It is a deeper sentiment and interacts with innate character traits. Still, there are many unanswered questions. Is hope in part genetically determined and, as such, a lasting trait that is resistant to negative shocks? The "joy in the struggle" phrase above comes to mind. Or, like several of the Big Five personality traits, is it more malleable over time? Hope relates to aspirations, but aspirations are tied to specific goals. Hope is the loftier concept, the broader and less defined objectives that specific aspirations aim toward. Is hope eroded when aspirations are not met?

---

1 Safford (2004). Reproduced with kind permission of Victoria Safford.

Why write a book on hope *and* despair and not just one or the other? Lack of hope is not a complete definition of despair, nor is lack of despair a complete definition of hope. Yet they are intricately linked. There are precise definitions of each in the psychology and psychiatry literatures; I am building from these with an emphasis on the definition of agency (which implicitly includes resilience) being integral to hope.[2] As a scholar, I think it is important to clarify these definitions. As a private citizen, I am increasingly concerned that the extent of despair in the United States threatens to undermine our civil society, our public health, and even our democracy.

What we do know is that hope matters to future outcomes. My starting point for this book is what I have learned from my research on the links between hope and future outcomes, and the channels by which that occurs (Graham et al. 2004; Graham and Pinto 2019; and O'Connor and Graham 2019). We know that hope is largely a positive trait that helps individuals manage—and even appreciate—life's challenges. Hope is particularly important for those who have less means and advantages with which to navigate those challenges.

Indeed, one of my most consistent yet counterintuitive findings is that the most disadvantaged populations are often more hopeful and resilient than more privileged ones, such as the happy peasants and frustrated achievers I found in Peru over twenty years ago (Graham and Pettinato 2002) and, more recently, my findings on high levels of optimism among low-income African Americans compared to despair among low-income whites in the United States (Graham and Pinto 2019). It is not clear if it is just optimism or hope in each instance, but the resilience of the respective populations and some more recent research on the longer-term outcomes of the latter suggest it is more likely hope than optimism.

---

2 As in the case of "hope springs eternal in the human breast," from Alexander Pope's *An Essay on Man* (1733).

Hope is central to the concept of recovery from mental disorders. Karl Menninger (1995) identified hope as integral to the profession of psychiatry—important for initiating therapeutic change and a willingness to learn and improving personal well-being. The psychiatric literature offers at least three reasons why hope is an important variable in mental health practice. First, it is both a trigger of the recovery process and a maintaining factor. Second, it is central to the concept of resilience. Third, it is central to human adaptation and psychotherapeutic change, consistently identified by both patients and therapists as a key factor in psychotherapy.[3] Nevertheless, the concept itself, as well as its clinical and research implications, has received little attention in psychiatry, a field in which the presence or absence of hope may have especially profound consequences.[4]

I am not a psychiatrist or a psychologist, and I have much to learn. I come from the perspective of an economist who studies well-being, a concept that encompasses both hope and despair as extremes. In studying despair and related deaths in the United States in recent years, and comparing that to my earlier work on happiness, hope, and resilience among the poor in poor places, I am increasingly aware of lack of hope as a major problem in the United States. Of course, this does not apply to all people, but it is a growing and evident trait among the increasing numbers of people in despair in the United States. How and why does the wealthiest country in the world have so much despair? What are we missing?

Despair in the United States today is a barrier to reviving our labor markets and productivity. It jeopardizes our well-being, longevity, families, and communities—and even our national security. While the COVID-19 pandemic was

---

3 See Bonney (2008); Ong et al. (2006); Hayes (2007); and Schrank et al. (2008).
4 Schrank et al. (2011).

a fundamental shock, it merely exacerbated an already growing problem of despair.

This despair results in part from the decline of the white working class. It contributes to our decreasing geographic mobility and has political spillovers, such as the recent increase in far-right radicalization. At the same time, other population groups are also suffering, for different reasons. Over the past few years, for instance, suicides increased among minority youths, and overdoses increased among Black urban males in 2019–20 (starting from a lower level than whites but at a higher rate of increase), in large part due to the introduction of fentanyl, a particularly lethal opioid derivative, but also due to rising anxiety rates (still coupled with optimism among many) that came with the COVID-19 shock.

There are many underlying longer-term problems: joblessness and/or labor force drop out; drug addiction; poor health; lack of adequate safety nets and affordable medical care; and inadequate publicly available education for rapidly changing labor markets. All of these are policy problems that have viable solutions, and yet none are, in my view, solvable without hope. And unresolved despair is already evident in the rising numbers of deaths of despair, in our high levels of labor force dropout, and in our divided and radicalized politics.

One reason for the despair is that the costs of "failure" are so high in the United States. The prohibitive cost of health care—and the links between employment status and health insurance when joblessness is at an all-time high—is a key factor eroding hope in the face of failure. Despair describes the plight of many who are ambivalent about whether they live or die. The latter impacts risk-taking, as in behaviors that jeopardize health and longevity.[5] Entire communities can

---

5 I thank Nancy Hey for her thoughts on this topic, as well as her reference to the following on risky behaviors: https://whatworkswell-being.org/blog/happy-people-wear-seat-belts-risk-taking-and-well-being/.

experience this helplessness, especially when confronted with difficult choices and change. They are often stuck in two worlds: one in which the old ways that held meaning are disappearing and the other in which the changes needed to succeed seem impossible in the absence of support. Death (slow or fast) becomes the simplest choice to stop the pain. Drug use and suicide are internal expressions of this, while expressed misery, frustration, and anger—which have security implications when widespread—are external ones.

A fundamental point of inquiry in my research is whether hope can be restored in populations where it has been lost. This is particularly important for the next generation. The children of those already in despair need hope and a vision for the future to avoid the fate of their parents.

In the context of rapidly changing labor markets in the low- and medium-skill job arena, a traditional high school education alone is no longer enough to make a decent living or to have stable employment. And while certain education options other than a college education can make a decent job achievable in the labor markets of tomorrow, without hope—and mentors who can support that hope and explain available options—many in the next generation will end up without the necessary skills necessary to do so. My surveys of low-income adolescents in Missouri, discussed in detail in chapter 5, make this sad reality all too clear. Understanding how to introduce hope into these same populations, so that they believe in and invest in their futures, is a critical part of the solution to avoiding another generation in despair.

Objectives of the Book

This is an unusual topic for economists, and my research is, by definition, exploratory. I seek to expand on established parameters and use a mix of econometric analysis of large N survey data and in-depth field surveys. I also draw from what we know from other disciplines, especially psychology. My aim in this book, though, is to demonstrate the potential benefits of incorporating hope into economic analysis, including into the analysis of human well-being. While this is relatively unknown territory, the empirical evidence that demonstrates that hope can improve people's life outcomes and that despair can destroy them is robust enough to merit a deeper exploration.

There are many unanswered questions. For example, what causes what? Do the same genes that are linked to innate levels of well-being—such as the 5-HTTLPR serotonin transmitter gene—also link to hope? Does hope result in individuals having more positive interactions with their environments, in the same way that those with higher levels of the serotonin transmitter have more positive interactions, thereby supporting the transmission of this gene across generations?[6] How persistent are these within-person psychosocial traits? Are they resilient to negative shocks as individuals navigate their environments? Are they persistent after young adulthood, like IQ, or malleable into the older ages, like the Big Five?[7] Although we are far from answering these questions, our initial research results are provocative.

We also know—from our research and that of others—that culture and community play a role in the persistence of these traits across certain population cohorts. In the United States, African Americans, particularly low-income ones, are more optimistic than low-income brackets of other races, and the gap is particularly large compared to low-income whites. De Neve and colleagues (2012) also find that African Americans have higher levels of the functional polymorphism on the serotonin transmitter gene (5-HTTLPR) than whites, His-

---

6 De Neve et al. (2012).
7 See Borghans et al. (2008); Benjamin et al. (2012); and Heckman and Kautz (2012).

panics, or Asians. The same research finds that 5-HTTLPR is protective of stress leading to depression, which may help explain the remarkable resilience in this same racial cohort. While these findings are new and remain to be tested further, they are potentially part of the explanation.

Our most recent work finds that African American optimism and resilience—and the gap compared to other groups—held even during the COVID-19 pandemic, which disproportionately affected them.[8] Our survey research—and that of some others—also finds that African Americans are more likely to believe in the value of higher education than low-income whites, even though it is often more difficult for the former group to achieve it.

Latin Americans, meanwhile, are consistently more cheerful and optimistic than respondents in other regions with similar levels of income, traits that persist when controlling for a host of other potentially confounding factors, such as religion, crime rates, and inequality. Our surveys of Peruvian young adults in low-income communities find remarkably high levels of hope and education aspirations, which yield better future outcomes in the education, health, and social arenas.[9]

While generalizing about particular population cohorts and/or races is difficult and often inaccurate, a driving channel is the high levels of hope among these two groups and the strong links it has to one's determination to surmount obstacles (such as discrimination) and to improve one's situation. As such, it is a concept that also includes agency and resilience.

Another question is whether hope (and optimism) are always good things. On the one hand, hope and resilience

8 https://www.brookings.edu/research/well-being-and-mental-health-amid-covid-19-differences-in-resilience-across-minorities-and-whites/.

9 This is discussed in detail in chapter 3 and in Graham and Ruiz-Pozuelo (2022).

are critical tools for navigating adversity. Certain well-being markers, such as high levels of cheerfulness and daily happiness in the face of deep poverty, may preserve mental health. But on the other hand, those qualities are associated with low expectations and adaptation to bad institutional arrangements and conditions, such as high levels of discrimination and high rates of crime and corruption.[10] Can we test this empirically?

Related to this question, which is also noted in the poem above, is whether hope for the long term—and associated aspirations—is different from raw optimism. While this is a difficult question to answer, we have explored it to the extent we could. The same low-income African American respondents who reported high levels of optimism also reported low levels of satisfaction with their finances and the cities they lived in, suggesting this is not a "Pollyanna" effect. In our Peru surveys, meanwhile, we tested three different types of aspirations—educational, occupational, and geographic (migration to better opportunities)—among our young adult respondents and found that hope and aspirations operate differently from raw optimism and reflect differences in traits like self-esteem, impatience, and willingness to partake in risky behaviors. Raw optimism has a less consistent association with our outcome measures. The work of some other scholars, discussed in the next chapter, corroborates these findings.

We also used the longitudinal nature of the Peru study to see how persistent aspirations were within individuals over the three-year time period, when our respondents ranged in age from eighteen to twenty-one. While a relatively short period of time, it is also a time of change, in which adolescents are transitioning into adulthood and make many critical choices that can permanently influence their futures.

10 Graham (2011).

We found that aspirations were indeed "sticky" and that our respondents with high aspirations were on track to complete their education goals by our second round. Finally, in addition to exploring how aspirations varied with individual characteristics, including the ones noted above, we had extensive information on their childhood experiences and the characteristics of their households—including the nature of their relationships with their parents—and could explore how those affected their hopes for the future.

The frame for this study of hope is the economics of well-being, a field I have contributed to from early on. It has developed from the study of the determinants of reported happiness across individuals and countries to a more sophisticated science, which incorporates approaches from several disciplines, including the biological sciences, and explores the interaction between innate traits and the environment in determining well-being. We now measure several distinct dimensions of well-being, ranging from experienced/hedonic well-being (momentary) to evaluative (over the life course) to eudaimonic (meaning and purpose in life). A growing body of research also explores what well-being causes in addition to what causes well-being.[11]

We have less experience measuring hope. For the most part, we have relied on available questions in large N surveys, such as the Gallup data.[12] In the Gallup data, right after the Cantril ladder of life question, which asks respondents to compare their life to the best possible life they can imagine on an eleven-step ladder, there is a follow-up question that asks respondents to place where they think their life will be in five years on the same scale. While it may be an imperfect question, it seems to capture two elements of hope: the

---

11 Graham, Eggers, and Sukhtankar (2004); De Neve and Oswald (2012). More of the well-being literature is reviewed in chapter 2.

12 I received the Gallup data in my capacity as an (unpaid) senior scientist there.

belief that things will be better in the future and the ability to do something about that future. The first is part of the question; the second is suggested by our findings, which are that people with higher scores on the future ladder tend to do better in the years following their interviews. While this may be due to realistic expectations, that does not explain the high scores of deprived populations, such as low-income African Americans.

Other hope questions simply ask respondents if they have hope for the future, on a similar if not exact response scale. Hope for the future is also often used as one in a series of questions to see if adolescents are depressed or not, such as the Center for Epidemiologic Studies Depression Scale, which asks respondents if they felt hopeful for the future all the time, often, some of the time, or none of the time. Regardless of the question differences, the patterns in the respondents' future behaviors suggest they all capture the same concept. And, indeed, in our own surveys of low-income adolescents in Peru and Missouri, we included two different hope questions (the Cantril ladder question and the twelve-item scale that Abler et al. [2017] developed for adolescents in South Africa) and found similar response patterns for both.

My recent research has explored how and why well-being—and well-being inequality—matters to individual outcomes, as well as to the consequences of low levels of well-being, particularly the absence of hope. That work was initially triggered by experiences working in Peru and other developing countries and noting upon each return that poverty in the United States seemed so much more hopeless than in places that were more deprived in a material sense. This seems to have roots in our high and increasingly higher levels of inequality of income and opportunity. The same strong individual work ethic that underlies the American Dream also includes tolerance for high levels of inequality and often stigmatizes the poor and those who fall behind.

I began my empirical exploration by comparing how levels of well-being—in addition to income and opportunity—were shared across the rich and poor in the United States. My findings were stark. I found that the gaps between the rich and the poor on reported stress and smiling were twice as large in the United States than Latin America, with the U.S. poor being the group least likely to smile and the most likely to be stressed of the four groups. And the gaps in believing that hard work would get you ahead were much larger between the poor and the rich in the United States than Latin America, where there was no significant income differential in these responses (Graham 2017).

I delved deeper into differences across income/race groups in the United States, with a focus on the poor groups. This was in 2015, approximately the time of the St. Louis and Baltimore riots, and prior to our awareness of the deaths of despair among less-than-college-educated whites. I found that poor Blacks were three times more likely to be higher up on an eleven-point optimism scale than poor whites, with Hispanics in between. Poor Blacks were also half as likely to report stress on a given day than poor whites and less likely to report pain. Given that the objective conditions of the former are far worse, the findings reflected resilience as much as reality. These results were *not* a result of reporting or scale bias, as the same low-income Black respondents were more negative than whites when assessing their financial situations and living conditions.

I explored the historical and cultural underpinnings of these differences. The role of community is an important part of the resilience story for minorities. Baptist churches—which tend to emphasize the collective rather than the individual—are an essential part of many African American communities. Extended families and Catholic churches play a similar role for Hispanics. Many of these communities were built on empathy, as minorities have collectively had to battle a system of discrimination and injustice. Even when we conducted research on the ill-being of prime-aged men out of the labor force (OLF)—a desperate group with high levels of opioid addition and poor objective health indicators—we found that African American males stand out *within* this group for taking pride in giving back to their communities (Graham and Pinto 2021).

It is difficult to measure the influence of community precisely. For example, we find that African Americans are the racial group most likely to report that religion is important in their lives. Although we control for religiosity in our regressions to make sure it is not driving our optimism findings, there are many unobservable qualities related to religiosity that we are unable to control for. It is quite likely that these matter to the story of optimism and resilience—and its grounding in broader communities.

Once the deaths of despair data came out (Case and Deaton 2015), it became clear that these deaths were more prevalent among low-income whites than other racial groups. We matched the patterns in our data on lack of hope, and stress and worry, and the county-level data from the Centers for Disease Control and Prevention (CDC) on these deaths. We found strong associations between our markers—and lack of hope in particular—and propensity to deaths of despair, at the level of individuals, race, and place (Graham and Pinto 2019). Those patterns remain robust until the present, demonstrating the potential of well-being metrics as useful tools for taking societies' temperatures, so to speak, and providing warning indicators of potential crises.[13]

Our latest work explores the mental health effects of COVID-19 and the impact on trends of deaths of despair (we are using EMS first-responder data until updated CDC data is

---

13 See, for example, https://www.brookings.edu/interactives/wellbeing -interactive/.

available). We find an almost doubling of overdoses and related deaths and a smaller increase in suicide deaths (Dobson, Graham, Hua, and Pinto 2022).[14] What is remarkable, though, is the persistence of African American optimism and resilience—even during the pandemic. Low-income African Americans remain the most hopeful race/income cohort and report better mental health than their white and Hispanic counterparts.[15] While minorities did report an increase in anxiety and reported depression in 2020 compared to 2019, this increase did not translate into a decrease in reported hope levels.

These differentials in hope seem to transfer into different belief structures. Low-income African Americans and Hispanics are more likely to believe in the value of higher education than low-income whites, for example. Recent work on Historically Black Colleges and Universities (HBCUs), which disproportionately serve low-income minorities, shows that students achieve high performance with far fewer resources than their counterparts in the public and private sectors, in part because they play a critical role in providing role models and mentors who help bolster hope and self-esteem.[16] Our surveys of low-income adolescents in white and Black neighborhoods in Missouri, meanwhile, find that though graduation rates are lower at predominantly African American schools, those graduating students are more likely to pursue higher education than whites.

Standing in sharp contrast to this hope and resilience are the high levels of despair—and related deaths—among

14 These trends seem puzzling, but it may well be that intentional overdose deaths replaced some suicides. In addition, as the highest suicide rate is for older men (particularly white males) and many older men died of COVID-19 in 2020, that may also have affected the suicide rate. Our EMS data analysis aligns closely to the trends in the preliminary data on mortality for 2020 that the CDC released in July 2021. See Dobson et al. (2021).

15 Graham et al. (2022), *PLOS one*.

16 https://www.brookings.edu/blog/brown-center-chalkboard/2021/01/18/when-it-comes-to-student-success-hbcus-do-more-with-less/.

less-than-college-educated whites in declining communities across the country. These high levels of despair are most prominent in places that were previously hubs for manufacturing and mining firms. Labor force dropout is high in these (largely white) communities—and typically higher than the nationwide average of 20% of prime-aged males out of the labor force.

Our research finds that this group has poor mental and physical health and high levels of opioid consumption. A higher percentage of prime-aged males out of the labor force remain in their parents' homes or census tracts than other labor force groups, one reason for the declining levels of geographic mobility in the United States.[17] With poor health and no hope or aspirations for the future, these individuals are unlikely to move to where jobs are, even if they are reasonably close. They are the starkest manifestation of the decline of the working class and seem to be vulnerable to media manipulation and to the priming of nativist and racist messaging.[18] These patterns suggest that, to solve this public health crisis, understanding hope is as critical as understanding despair (this is documented in detail in our Brookings report on despair and recovery, which I led in 2021).[19]

A note of caution is the possibility that optimists simply mispredict or are perennial Pollyannas.[20] Or they may just be adapting to difficult circumstances because they have no other choice. Much of my earlier work on the happiness of the very poor in poor places suggested this to be a common phenomenon—something I termed "the happy peasant versus frustrated achiever problem" almost two decades ago (Graham 2009).

17 Graham and Pinto (2021).
18 Edsall (2021a; 2021b).
19 https://www.brookings.edu/research/addressing-americas-crisis-of -despair-and-economic-recovery/.
20 Odermatt and Stutzer (2019); Schwandt (2016).

Yet now that more sophisticated methods allow us to distinguish between momentary moods and sentiments—such as contentment—and cognitive life-course evaluations, we find major differences across these types of scores in the same cohorts. The very poor may report to be "happy" in the former sense, perhaps because they had seen their friends or had enough to eat that day, but when asked about their life satisfaction as a whole or other evaluative questions, the same respondents scored much lower, scores that accurately reflected their lack of ability to make choices about the kinds of lives they want to lead. As such, the "happy peasants" may have been happy in the momentary sense but not with their overall lives. This is distinct from hope, although, as I mentioned above, the high levels of resilience among poor Peruvians and their strong belief in education and better lives for their children suggest that their responses also reflect some elements of hope. We did not ask specific questions that explored their levels of hope at the time since the study was conducted in 1990, when the well-being field was in its early stages.

More recently, my findings—including on hope leading to better outcomes and longer lives, and on the terrible outcomes associated with despair—suggest that, on average, hope is not a fleeting trait or a misprediction about the future; it serves as a driving force in life outcomes (O'Connor and Graham 2019; Graham and Ruiz-Pozuelo 2021). Inevitably there may still be eternal optimists who are out of touch with reality, but they are likely the exception rather than the rule.

A key question of this book is what can we do with this knowledge? Can we restore hope in populations where it has been lost? Are the lessons from optimistic and resilient populations generalizable to other populations? Can interventions enhance hope?

We have some evidence that the answer is positive. Haushofer and Fehr (2014), for example, found that simple interventions in very poor places—such as providing households with a small asset like a cow—resulted in better outcomes a year later, with the driving channel being hope. Hall, Zhao, and Shafir (2013) conducted an experiment in soup kitchens in Trenton, New Jersey, and found that participants who had been triggered to think of a time when they felt good about themselves outperformed those who had not received a prompt in a simple game-playing setting, with the difference being the participants' increased effort in the games. (Given the setting, the authors do not have data on the duration of the positive effects of their intervention.) More recently, a broader set of well-being interventions, as in the work of the What Works Centre for Wellbeing in the U.K. and the Santa Monica Well-Being Project, have shown that simple activities that get isolated respondents into purposeful activities in the community can have major impacts on individual and community well-being.

All of this points to the need to explore hope's causal properties, its potential as a distinct well-being dimension, and whether it can be learned in populations and places where it is lacking.

Guidepost to the Book

Chapter 2 provides a brief review of the study of well-being in economics and discusses the potential of hope as a separate and new well-being dimension. I also describe some new work (much of it my own) on using well-being metrics to better understand the causes and patterns in death of despair. I use my last Princeton Press book, *Happiness for All: Unequal Hopes and Lives in Pursuit of the American Dream*, as a starting point for discussing the inequality of well-being— and how that relates to the stark decline of the working class in the United States. I then review new empirical evidence from my recent work, using well-being metrics as a tracking tool for vulnerability to despair-related deaths and the recent experiences with using well-being interventions to improve the lives of the isolated and desperate. I have collaborated in many of these latter efforts. I also introduce important factors that we know less about, such as differences in communities and cultures across races (which in part explain the large well-being gaps across them) and what we know and do not know about the generalizability of the positive lessons from some communities and cultures to other ones, where hope has been lost. I also review some of the new literatures on the genetic determinants of hope and the neuroscience of despair.

Chapter 3 summarizes the research on the hopes and aspirations of low-income young adults in Lima, Peru. The panel nature of the data allows us to explore how hope leads to better outcomes and the relative roles of within person traits—which are persistent in our data, versus the socioeconomic and community environments that these young adults live in. It shows how different kinds of aspirations—educational, occupational, and for migration opportunities—influence behaviors and outcomes in different ways, and the role of parental or mentor support in that process. I also address the question of how enduring aspirations are in the face of negative shocks. While our time period is not long enough to answer this definitively, our findings clearly point to persistence in aspirations and their role in better long-term outcomes.

Chapter 4 focuses on the field surveys of young adults in low-income Black and white communities in St. Louis County, Missouri—a central heartland state in the United States (which shares borders with seven other states!). These surveys include essentially the same questions as the Peru survey but adapted for the U.S. context—and for the COVID-19 experience. While we only have one round of surveys available at the writing of this book, they provide extensive background and contextual information on the respondents and their future aspirations. We also have the support of the local school superintendents to provide us with broader information on the typical trajectories of students with the same socioeconomic and racial characteristics of our respondents, such as the above-cited school data on Black graduates pursuing high school at a higher rate than white ones. I also discuss the differences across races in the roles of parents as mentors and in supporting their children's aspirations.

The discussion helps inform our understanding of the crisis of despair and vulnerability in our society and attempt to provide some glimmers of hope for addressing it. It also highlights the pressing need for low-income young adults to have hope and a vision for the future to make the investments they need to participate in challenging labor markets (now even more uncertain due to the COVID-19 shock) to avoid the fate of the high percentage of prime-aged adults without a college education who have dropped out of the labor force and have high rates of despair and associated behaviors.

Chapter 5 builds on all of this and asks the difficult question of whether hope can be restored in places where it has been lost. I posit that the lessons from the hope and resilience of deprived minority populations can be applicable in other ones, but I also discuss the challenges of doing so. I provide detail on successful interventions to enhance well-being work among the isolated and address the additional efforts necessary to use the same approaches to make more lasting changes to people's outlooks for the future.

Chapter 6 summarizes the findings and makes the case for establishing and using hope as a distinct well-being dimension, in addition to the hedonic, evaluative, and eudaimonic dimensions, because of its direct channel to enhancing future outcomes. I make a related case for increasing the inclusion of questions about hope in data and analysis in economics and possibly other social sciences, as well as in policy discussions.

While hope is not a usual topic of either economics or policy discussions, our society's high levels of despair—now worsened by the COVID-19 shock—have led to new attempts to measure depression, anxiety, and other kinds of ill-being. Such questions are increasingly included in surveys conducted by agencies such as the Federal Reserve, the Bureau of Labor Statistics, the U.S. Department of Health and Human Services, and the CDC (I have been asked to review many of these). I try to make the case that better understanding the determinants of hope—which also entail assessing trends in hope as well as in ill-being in current surveys—is a critical antidote to the increase in these trends.

Finally, I conclude with a discussion of why addressing despair in our society—and restoring hope in populations where it has been lost—is critical to our country's future. Despair is currently eroding our civil society and democracy, damaging our health and longevity, and serving as a major drag on our society's productivity and potential. There are many pragmatic and feasible ways to address this problem. Yet, without hope, people are unlikely to participate in them and recover. As such, I offer an unusual but critical solution to the problem. While it resembles raw optimism, its basis in the tools offered by economics, psychology, and other social and medical disciplines attributes to it the additional agentic properties that are so important in distinguishing hope from "the prudent gates of Optimism, nor the stalwart, boring gates of Common Sense; nor the strident gates of Self-Righteousness, which creak on shrill and angry hinges . . . nor the cheerful, flimsy garden gate of 'Everything is gonna be all right.'"

CHAPTER 2

Hope, Genes, Environment, and the Brain

WHAT WE KNOW AND DO NOT KNOW

"He who has not hoped can never despair."

—George Bernard Shaw

Hope is the subject of many writings, both colloquial and academic (economics excepted, until recently). Former president Barack Obama's *The Audacity of Hope* and similar hope-inspired titles have appeared on book covers for years, including my recent *Happiness for All? Unequal Hopes and Lives in Pursuit of the American Dream*.

Yet do we really know what hope is? Are our conceptions of hope concrete or is it just a wise intuition? While there are many related definitions, there is no real consensus on a definition or on why hope is so important. At the same time, there is wide recognition that lack of hope is at the root of many societal problems, and certainly those we are experiencing in the United States today.

There is now a nascent academic literature on hope and its causal properties. My research in economics—and that of a few others, cited below—finds that hope is associated with better future outcomes in many populations. This is in part due to the future-oriented agentic properties associated with hope. Optimism, in contrast, is more open-ended and at times naively positive about the future.

As Scott Barry Kaufman (2021) writes, "tragic optimism" is the search for meaning during the inevitable tragedies of human existence and is better for us than simply avoiding darkness and trying to "stay positive." Optimism is a general belief that things will turn out all right; hope is a conviction that one can act to make things better in some way. As such, there are hopeless optimists and hopeful pessimists (Brooks 2021).

One of the reasons for the emergence of this literature is the growing evidence that people with higher levels of subjective well-being fare better over the life course, typically living longer, performing better in the labor market, and having better social lives. Hope is implicitly part of well-being; it is a reported cognitive emotion and an evaluation of how life could be in the future. Yet, in comparison to the increasingly voluminous body of economics and other research on the other dimensions of subjective well-being, the literature on hope in economics is sparse. Hope is not considered a distinct dimension of well-being. The more I understand it and its causal properties, though, the more I believe it *should* be a separate dimension—and perhaps the most critical one in a life-course sense (for detailed definitions of all the dimensions, see Stone and Mackie 2013).

The subjective well-being dimension we know the most about is evaluative well-being. It is typically captured by a life satisfaction question in which respondents evaluate their lives in a general sense. The determinants of life satisfaction are remarkably similar across people, countries, and cultures around the world. Income matters—not least because those who are destitute are far less able to choose the kinds of lives they lead—but with the typical diminishing marginal returns at the top of the income scale (with some outliers). Health matters as much if not more than income, while freedom, creativity, employment, and social relationships (with the latter having two-way causality, as happier people are more likely to make friends and to marry) are also important factors. Age has a U-shaped relationship with life satisfaction in most of the world's population, with the low point at middle age and then rising with age, controlling for income and health, until roughly the mid-seventies. Some of this is driven by selection bias, as happier people tend to live longer than unhappy people.[1]

The findings about what higher levels of life satisfaction can cause are growing. In addition to living longer, happier people are more productive, less likely to take up behaviors that risk their futures, such as smoking and not wearing seatbelts, and more likely to volunteer, be altruistic, trust others, and to seek jobs that give them purpose and autonomy rather than just income alone.[2]

Hedonic well-being, in contrast, reflects momentary moods and daily experience rather than a cognitive assessment. It captures emotions ranging from contentment and smiling, to stress, anxiety, anger, and frustration. Unlike life satisfaction, it cannot be measured on a one-dimensional scale, running from zero to ten. Negative and positive emotions must be measured separately, as contentment, for example, is not the positive analogue to stress. And while positive emotions and actions such as smiling and contentment track closely with one another *and* with life satisfaction, the negative emotions, particularly anger, do not.[3]

Hedonic well-being is much less correlated with income than life satisfaction. After a certain point, more money will not make your moods better or make you enjoy your time with friends more, while more money allows people to make more choices in their lives, beyond meeting basic needs. In

---

1 For general reviews of this literature, see Blanchflower and Oswald (2004); Clark (2018); Easterlin (2021); Frey and Stutzer (2002); and Graham (2009).

2 De Neve and Oswald (2012); Graham et al. (2004); Helliwell et al. (2018); and Nikolova and Cnossen (2021).

3 Stone and Mackie (2013).

addition, as hedonic well-being captures momentary moods rather than life chances and choices, it has fewer causal properties (although high levels of stress are associated with worse long-term health outcomes).[4]

Eudaimonic well-being, which explicitly captures Aristotle's conceptualization of happiness as having a purposeful and meaningful life, has similar determinants to evaluative well-being, with income, health, and employment—all factors that give people the agency to choose the kinds of lives they want to lead—being critical variables. Yet the role of country-specific variance is one area in which eudaimonic well-being differs from evaluative well-being. What individuals consider a meaningful and purposeful life seems to be more influenced by specific cultural traits than life satisfaction.[5]

Well-being metrics are increasingly being incorporated into policy in many countries—such as the U.K, New Zealand, Canada, and even in some new official surveys in the United States—as a complement to other measures of progress, such as GNP indicators, and as a tool to take society's temperature, so to speak, in terms of stress, anger, optimism, and despair. Some countries, such as the U.K. and New Zealand, are also incorporating the metrics into their treasuries and other government operations to set priorities and to inform cost-benefit analysis.[6]

There are also local-level efforts that use the metrics to design and evaluate interventions to deal with individual and community-level despair. These efforts have a great deal of promise, but they also need to be introduced cautiously; care needs to be given to explaining their nature and purpose, as well as the scales upon which assessments are based. It is extremely important to emphasize that well-being measurement

4 Kahneman and Deaton (2010); Kubzansky et al. (2014).
5 Nikolova and Graham (2015).
6 For an excellent discussion of the pros—and cons—of using such an approach, see O'Donnell and Oswald (2015).

is not a tool for the government to tell people how to be happy, but rather a tool for using people's self-reports about their welfare as an input into the policy process that prioritizes society's well-being in addition to economic objectives.

As noted above, our knowledge of and literature on hope is far less developed, even in the fields of psychology and psychiatry. There is a nascent consensus, though, that hope has cognitive, emotional, and agentic properties that are important to future-oriented behaviors and that distinguish it from associated dimensions such as optimism, aspirations, and expectations. And if, indeed, hope has a strong channel to people's future outcomes, then we need to know more about it if societies are going to use well-being metrics as policy tools.

Hope in the Literature

Pleeging et al. (2021) make the point that both hope and subjective well-being are multidimensional concepts comprising emotion (such as anticipation and affect), cognition (such as expectations and satisfaction), and motivation. Their findings, based on both meta-analysis and on a nationally representative sample of the U.S. population, show that positive expectations are only weakly associated with all domains of subjective well-being, while cognitive and emotional hope are much more so. They conclude that the more passive elements of positive expectations—just thinking that things will be positive in the future—are less important in these relationships than having a more agentic hopeful disposition. Indeed, much of the other literature on hope, discussed below, suggests that having a sense of agency rather than just positive—and at times naive—optimism distinguishes hope's causal links to better future outcomes.[7]

---

7 See also Schrank et al. (2011); Graham and Ruiz-Pozuelo (2022).

Beatrice Schrank and coauthors (2011) summarized the limited literature and extant knowledge on the concept of hope and its clinical and research implications in psychiatry. They note the lack of clarity on a definition, while at the same time the implicit consensus that the personal sense of hopefulness—or recovering it—is critical to mental health recovery of psychiatric patients. They propose a need for future research based on observational and intervention studies to increase our understanding of why and how hope is so central to this process. Perhaps not coincidentally, the nascent science of well-being has been fielding interventions for almost a decade to increase hope, particularly in distressed communities and populations where it has been lost (see examples in chapter 5).

Tyler VanderWeele and colleagues (Gallagher et al. 2020) note that the early proponents of positive psychology, most notably Richard Snyder, began conceptualizing hope as a positive motivational state that enables people to persevere toward goals and pathways. In a recent article, they find that hope has a significant association with long-term health outcomes via a variety of psychosocial processes such as emotional adjustment, positive affect, life satisfaction, sense of purpose, quality of life, and social support.[8] Conversely, low levels of hope—or hopelessness—are positively associated with higher risk of mental health problems such as anxiety, depression, and posttraumatic stress disorder (and hopelessness is now used as an item for depression assessment).

Based on data from the U.S. health and retirement study (N = 12,998 with a mean age of sixty-six), they found that a greater sense of hope was associated with better physical health and some health indicators, such as a reduced risk of all-cause mortality, fewer chronic conditions, lower cancer

8 Snyder (2000); Gallagher et al. (2020).

risk, fewer sleep problems, higher psychological well-being, lower psychological distress, and better social well-being.

Travis Lybbert and Bruce Wydick (2018), among the few economists to incorporate Snyder's approach in their work, also focus on hope's agentic properties and the ability to see—and take—different pathways to find a better future. They model hope as incorporating aspirations (goals), agency (self-efficacy), and pathways to change, and focus on interventions to help people get out of extreme poverty.

Alan Piper (2022) takes a different approach. Rather than focus on causal links to future outcomes, he examines the links between optimism (and pessimism) and current life satisfaction, based on data from the German Socioeconomic Panel. He finds that even controlling for anticipated events, such as marriage or divorce and the birth of a child, and for person fixed effects, there is a strong link between optimism about the future and current life satisfaction. The association is even stronger for pessimism and lower levels of life satisfaction. His findings make intuitive sense, in that those who believe their futures will be positive, or even better than now, are likely to have high levels of life satisfaction, and at the same time his findings suggest that personality traits are also at play.

A second perspective is offered by personality and social psychologists (and some economists) who believe that aspirations (which are integral to the definitions of hope above) are linked to but distinct from broad personality traits. The latter include traits like self-esteem, locus of control, and self-efficacy. Studies have shown that compared to measures of fluid intelligence such as IQ, personality traits are more likely to evolve over time and to interact with the environment well into middle age.[9] These personality traits, in turn, are known to predict future outcomes such as education

---

9 Almlund et al. (2011); Bandura et al. (2001); and Dercon and Singh (2013).

attainment, health, and labor as strongly as measures of cognitive ability.[10]

Heckman and Kautz (2012) use the term "personality traits" to describe the attributes that are not captured by measures of abstract reasoning power, such as IQ. These attributes have many names, including soft skills, personality traits, noncognitive skills, character, and socioemotional skills. These different names connote different properties. The term "traits" suggests a sense of permanence and possibly also of heritability, while the terms "skills" and "character" suggest they can be learned. Their empirical work suggests that both cognitive and personality traits can change and be changed over the life cycle but through different mechanisms and at different ages. Psychological traits—including hope—evolve until much later in life (middle age) in contrast to IQ, which does not change much after one's twenties.

Yet Heckman and Kautz also note that most studies of the role of personality traits in determining outcomes, by both psychologists and economists, neglect to include the role of a deeper set of preferences or goals, which can also be thought of as traits. Achieving such goals requires certain traits, such as intelligence or conscientiousness. Under this view, traits are developed through practice, investment, and habituation, which are influenced by incentives. The apparent stability of expressed traits across situations may be a consequence of the stability of the goals and incentives themselves. Studies that account for the endogeneity of investments, as in education, provide further evidence of the causal effect of education and cognitive and personality traits on outcomes. As such, human capital outcomes are at least in part endogenous to personality traits such as hope.

They rely on the so-called Big Five personality traits in their empirical work. These are conscientiousness, agreeableness,

---

10 Borghans et al. (2008); Heckman and Kautz (2012).

openness to experience, extroversion, and neuroticism/emotional stability. While these are largely stable over the life course, they can be influenced by experiences, parenting, and other things. The traits that we use in our survey—such as optimism, self-esteem, belief in hard work, mental states, impatience, and ability to make friendships—have many elements of these five traits.

Some related work by Ryon and Gleason (2014) on locus of control finds that it also evolves over the life course. They also find that locus of control was positively associated with positive health behaviors and that it predicted negative health symptoms. These results provide evidence for a social learning perspective on the development and maintenance of individuals' sense of control. The authors posit that locus of control should be considered both a state- and trait-level construct in future research.

Differences across Races, Cultures, and Populations

Our own research—and that of some others—finds large differences in the prevalence of hope—and its underlying traits—across people, races, and cultures. In the United States, for example, during these times of high levels of despair, a surprising and persistent finding is the high levels of hope among minorities—African Americans in particular—compared to high levels of despair among whites. The gaps between the two cohorts are the highest at low levels of income, even though African Americans are significantly more deprived in material and social justice terms than whites. This finding, meanwhile, is not a reflection of "tragic optimism" or Pollyanna-like beliefs. The same optimistic Black respondents report their financial and living situations to be far worse than the average. The gaps are also high at older ages. Young people tend to be more optimistic about the future than older ones (for obvious reasons) while older people tend to have higher levels of life satisfaction than younger people; yet African Americans are the only racial group in the United States that retains high optimism levels well into old age.[11]

Sergio Pinto and I first found this seeming paradox in our large N data work, based on Gallup data, which compared hope for the future—and attitudes about getting ahead via individual effort and hard work—across low-income racial cohorts.[12] We initially uncovered this paradox in 2015, prior to the release of Case and Deaton's seminal paper on our increasing mortality due to deaths of despair later that same year. Our work yielded high levels of optimism about the future among poor African Americans—at a time of widespread concern about police violence against African Americans and riots in the cities of St. Louis and Baltimore—in sharp contrast to low levels of hope and high levels of worry and stress among low-income whites, a finding that surprised us at first, but then seemed to mirror the actual mortality patterns in the deaths of despair data.

We proceeded to match our metrics of well-being and ill-being in our Gallup nationwide data at the level of individuals, races, and places—counties and Metropolitan Statistical Areas—with the trends in deaths from the CDC data for these kinds of deaths (suicide, drug overdoses, alcohol poisonings, and "unexplained accidental deaths") and found robust matches over the time period from 2010 to 2017.[13] Since then, we have also used different data sets to explore historical linkages. We have found that ill-being preceded increases in these kinds of deaths in the data from the Panel Study on Income Dynamics, beginning with a drop in the optimism of less-than-college-educated white males in the late 1970s—corresponding

---

11 On age trends and optimism, see Schwandt (2016); on optimism and age differences across race, see Graham (2017).

12 I get access to the data in my capacity as a senior scientist at Gallup.

13 Graham and Pinto (2019).

with the first wave of manufacturing decline. More recently, using the Behavioral Risk Factor Surveillance Survey beginning in 2006, we found that the percent of respondents reporting bad mental health days per county was positively associated with higher levels of deaths of despair several years later.[14] All this analysis points to the absence of hope among certain populations—primarily (but not only) less-than-college-educated whites—as a plausible causal channel underlying these tragic mortality trends.

Another factor related to lack of hope is a lack of purpose in life and an absence of desire or agency to change that. We explored in detail the state of prime-aged males in the United States—a growing and particularly vulnerable group. We found that they were much more likely than any other labor force cohort, including the unemployed, to have high levels of despair, poor objective health conditions and behaviors (including high levels of opioid addiction), high levels of reported pain (often a pathway into addiction), and little geographic mobility. They were, for example, much more likely to be living in their parents' homes or census tract than other adult cohorts and therefore much less able and willing to move to other places with more employment opportunities.

And, reflecting the racial paradox above, white prime-aged males displayed far worse health and well-being indicators than minority ones, and African American prime-aged males were significantly *more* likely to report that they desired to contribute to making their community better, and took pride in doing so.[15]

These racial differences—and the stark Black-white gaps in hope and optimism—are remarkably persistent and have remained unchanged in our data throughout the 2016 election and the following controversial presidency that resulted and,

14 O'Connor and Graham (2019); Dobson et al. (2022).
15 Graham and Pinto (2021).

even more remarkably, during COVID-19, a time when low-income African Americans were much more likely to contract and/or die from COVID-19 than other cohorts, in large part due to the nature of their jobs and living arrangements. While anxiety increased at the same time among African Americans during this period, it remained at much lower levels than whites.[16]

This work has been an important precursor to research I am currently conducting on the determinants and future implications of hope among diverse cohorts of adolescents. I conducted a first pilot survey in Peru in 2017, with a follow-up three years later, in collaboration with Julia Ruiz Pozuelo, a doctoral student in psychiatry at the University of Oxford, and via the implementation capacity and IRB of the Nutrition Research Institute in Lima.[17]

We found incredibly high levels of hope and associated aspirations for education among a cohort of poor adolescents—eighteen to nineteen years of age—in San Juan de Lurigancho, a large peri-urban settlement outside Lima. Even though not one of our respondents had a parent with a college education, 85% of them reported to want to pursue college or postgraduate education. Our follow-up yielded high levels of within-person persistence in aspirations, with 95% of our high-aspirations respondents on track to achieve their education goals three years later and far less likely than the average to have pursued behaviors that would jeopardize their futures, such as taking drugs or having unsafe sex. It was also important to have a supportive mentor—either in

16 Graham, Chung, et al. (2022).

17 For full disclosure, the IIN was founded by my father, a pediatrician, in 1962, the year I was born. I have been involved in it some way or another most of my life, including currently serving on the scientific advisory board. We implemented the survey via the IIN's field team and went through their IRB as part of the process. We are very grateful to Dr. Mary Penny, the director, for her guidance throughout this process.

the family or neighboring community—as well as to be in a culture with a strong belief in the value of education. The channel from hope to better outcomes, meanwhile, seems to be particularly important to agency and persistence in a context of deprivation and repeated negative shocks.[18] I provide more detail on this survey and its findings and implications in chapter 3.

As a parallel effort, I have also fielded surveys of low-income African American and white students in poor school districts in St. Louis, Missouri, again in the eighteen to nineteen age range. The surveys were fielded with the assistance of NORC, previously known as the National Opinion Research Center, at the University of Chicago. These surveys proved to be more administratively difficult than the Peru surveys due to COVID-19 and ultimately were fielded by mail rather than in person.

While I describe the details of the survey and findings in chapter 4, it is worth noting that the stark Black-white gap in hope appears here and is associated with different levels of educational aspirations. A large majority of Black respondents aim to pursue college or postgraduate education even though it is materially more difficult for them than for the white respondents—and typically have at least one parent or grandparent supporting them in those goals—echoing the Peru findings. In contrast, the white respondents have or want to finish high school and, at most, perhaps an additional year of technical education. Equally notable, they report that their parents do not support them in achieving higher levels of education.

This reflects, among other things, the decline of the narrative of individual effort being the key to success for the white working class of today, and there is no new narrative to replace it. As a result, there is a deep skepticism of higher

18 Graham and Ruiz-Pozuelo (2022).

education and "coastal elites." This decline and associated lack of hope is likely to leave their children as the next generation in despair. Without hope and the agency to pursue more education (and there are many forms of skill acquisition in addition to college), these young adults are unlikely to have the skills—including socioemotional and cognitive ones—to navigate and succeed in tomorrow's labor markets. This not only suggests a sad future for these students but is a force contributing to our increasingly divided society and polity.

More on the African American Hope Paradox

The explanations for this multifaceted paradox are complex and come from many scholars and disciplines. As noted above, our research finds that African Americans are the only racial group that retains high levels of optimism well into old age.[19] Most other cohorts have less hope for the future as they enter their older years, yet African Americans maintain steady levels. The explanations for this shed some light on the broader paradox. The late sociologist James Jackson, for example, attributed the trend among older Blacks to one of "shedding difficult roles," and that since Blacks had traditionally been stuck with inferior and unpleasant jobs, retirement was a relief and a source of hope for a better existence, no matter how short.[20]

Historian Nancy Isenberg describes the historical resilience of poor African Americans compared to poor whites and how, in the South in the postslavery period, plantation owners were more likely to hire poor Blacks than poor whites to work on the farms. The perception was that the former worked much harder and was less likely to get sick, suggestive

19 Graham (2017).
20 Personal conversation with Jackson at an NIA workshop in Orlando, Florida, November 2015.

of both African American resilience and of a less positive story, which is that there was a selection bias in the African Americans who survived slavery—survival of the fittest, so to speak.[21]

In a more recent history of the workers in the Bethlehem Steel mills in Baltimore, sociologist Andrew Cherlin describes how the Black workers—who came to the mills in the 1950s from North Carolina on a special program, lived in segregated housing, and were denied the same promotion opportunities as white workers, even after civil rights laws changed—still saved more and did better over time than their counterparts.[22] Indeed, after the mills closed, the adult children of the white workers tended to remain in Dundalk and to work in less desirable jobs in the gig economy while most of the children of the Black workers attended college and moved out of the neighborhood to better ones north of town. Equally important to the story, they tended to come back to the same neighborhood (the one where the HBO television series *The Wire* was filmed) to attend church and to give back to the community.

Davis and Wu (2014) find that inequality has different effects in Black communities versus white ones. While higher levels of median income within a social group have negative effects on the life satisfaction of whites, consistent with preferences for within group status, it has positive effects for African Americans, who see increased median income within their group, even if they have much lower levels than the median, as a positive signal that their community is doing better. This community solidarity-based signaling channel is stronger for those with lower levels of income and for stu-

21 Isenberg (2017).
22 Cherlin (2019).

dents, in keeping with the higher levels of optimism among low-income Blacks compared to the average.

The persistent hope for the future, belief in the value of education in getting ahead, and the strong role of community are factors that are evident in our data work above and in the surveys of low-income adolescents in both Peru and Missouri, and they are central to the concept of hope that frames this book. What stands out in contrast to the remarkable levels of hope among African Americans is the extent to which hope has been lost among low-income whites and what it will take to restore it.

While there are many related explanations, not least the permanent decline in the availability and quality of blue-collar jobs, one of them, which contrasts sharply with the resilience that stems from having to constantly overcome adversity, is the relative decline—in status and in economic stability—of this cohort. The long-held narrative—and underpinning of the American Dream—of the white working class was an individualistic belief that hard work gets you ahead and that those who fall behind do so because of lack of effort. But in the same way that the famous Horatio Alger myth omitted the important historical fact that Horatio had a benefactor, the "work hard, you get ahead" narrative also omitted the fact that whites had a distinct advantage over minorities in getting the available—and best—blue-collar jobs (as in the steel mills).

Low-income whites faced two different types of decline. The first: due to significant increases in income inequality and decreases in intergenerational mobility in the United States, the absolute differences in the earnings and lifestyles between low-income whites and wealthy whites increased and their chances of narrowing those gaps and of their children living better lives than them decreased. The second: a relative decline in the gaps—in income, education, and health—between them and the minority cohorts who they had traditionally done better than.[23]

While African Americans were also hit hard by the negative effects of manufacturing decline—in terms of unemployment, poverty, and family stability, among other things[24]—they were more accustomed to dealing with negative shocks. As such, it seems to have not undermined their overall narrative and sense of purpose. In addition, precisely because of this history of dealing with adversity, African Americans and other minority groups, such as Hispanics, built something that I have labeled "communities of empathy," which are informal safety nets based on community support systems—from extended families to churches—that help support those who fall behind, in contrast to the stigma the working white class attaches to poverty. An additional part of the white working-class narrative—the stable family that went along with the stable job—also disintegrated along with the jobs.

There are, of course, many other reasons underlying the decline of white hope: the opioid epidemic, the increase in obesity and other health conditions that can exacerbate physical and psychological pain, and the increasing divisions— and ultimately cultural rifts—between, on the one hand, the economically diverse and vibrant coasts of the country and other large metropolitan areas and, on the other, much of the heartland, with its declining economic activity and population density. There are countless other related explanations, such as the decline in civic activity and education, the decline in religious activity and in membership in associations such as Lion's

23 In a paper that provides a new method for disentangling "fair" inequality, which is due to fair rewards for skills and effort, and "unfair" inequality, which is due to persistent advantages for certain groups, Paul Hufe, Kavi Kanbur, and Andreas Peichle (2022) find that most of the significant inequality increases in the United States over the past few decades were driven by inequality and differences in parental education outcomes.

24 Gould (2021).

Clubs and rotary clubs, and the disintegration of marriage as a norm among low-income whites (while it has increased for the wealthy and educated). Finally, there is also the rise of social media and fake news eroding the financial and reputational foundation of unbiased and nonpolitical news outlets—and the consensus on truth that they represented.[25]

The African American paradox of hope also has some downsides. While it is not a Pollyanna mindset, it does at some level accept that there will always be injustice and that it is part and parcel of racial and cultural pride to overcome it. Suicide, for example, is much lower among African Americans than whites in part because the cultural stigma against it is so high. Indeed, the effect of depressive symptoms on the increased risk of all-cause mortality, which is high for whites, was not evident for Blacks until 2019–20, and remains at much lower levels than for whites.[26] Tiffany Ford (2021), meanwhile, has highlighted a related paradox for lower- and middle-income Black women. Also using Gallup data, she finds middle-income Black women are the most optimistic race/income cohort, but that optimism coexists with high levels of stress and of diseases like diabetes and heart ailments.[27]

Shervin Assari has written extensively on these topics and finds that because of the high levels of optimism and resilience among Blacks, both health and education do less to preserve their happiness/mental health than for whites.[28] He also notes that because Blacks already have higher levels of hope and resilience, it may modify the protective role that that socioeconomic status and health play regarding the link

25 On civil trends, see Putnam (2015) and Sawhill (2019). On the challenges to the truth and the integrity of the media, see Rauch (2021).

26 Dobson et al. (2022).

27 Through my user agreement, Ford had access to the Gallup data as my PhD student and graduate assistant at the time.

28 Assari (2017).

between depressive systems and mortality over a long period of time. A forthcoming study in *Preventive Medicine* found that high levels of optimism are protective of mortality for African American men but not for women, for example, controlling for sociodemographic factors and depressive conditions. This is, indeed, a paradox that needs more explanation.

Believing this narrative may be more difficult for more educated and wealthier young African Americans, and this may reflect in the recent increase in suicide among educated minority teens.[29] Assari's studies show that living in a white neighborhood as a high-income African American adolescent seems to worsen preexisting depressive conditions. As these youths become more educated and aware, they may also realize the extent to which glass ceilings still exist for African Americans.

Questions emerge: When does hope reflect resilience and agency? And when is hope just optimism (perhaps tragic) reflecting adaptation? An insight comes from the work of McIntosh et al. (2021), who find that racial and ethnic minorities, including African Americans and Hispanics/Latinos, indicate lower tolerance to psychological distress (DT) and lower secular hope, yet endorse more religious and spiritual hope than their non-Hispanic White (NHW) counterparts.[30] Whether racial-ethnic minorities derive greater benefit from nonsecular hope on the tolerance of psychological distress remains unclear.

McGrath et al. (2021) analyzed self-reported endorsements of religious/spiritual (R/S) hope, secular hope, DT, and several other psychosocial, R/S, and sociodemographic variables in a nationwide survey of persons aged over eighteen years (N = 2875) identifying as Black (14.2%), Hispanic (15.4%), or NHW (67.3%). Overall, higher levels of both religious/spiritual

29 Assari et al. (2018).
30 McIntosh et al. (2021).

hope and secular hope predicted greater DT. In turn, greater DT was associated with lower psychosomatic distress. An unanswered question is whether religious/spiritual hope reflects agency and resilience among minorities or whether it reflects naive optimism. The other trends in the data suggest it is the former.[31]

Genes and Brains

There is indeed a genetic and neuroscience element to the roots of hope and other forms of well-being, although this is relatively uncharted and potentially controversial territory. Some of the earliest work (Caspi et al. 2003) based on a prospective longitudinal study of a nationally representative birth cohort in the United States explored why negative life events result in depression in some cohorts and not others. They found that a polymorphism in the serotonin transmitter 5-HTTLPR gene played a strong role, as it mitigated the effect of early life events on later-life depression. Those with at least one long allele of the polymorphism were less likely to have depressive symptoms, diagnosed depression, and suicidality later in life—in the face of negative shocks early on—than those with two short alleles. Their study is suggestive of genetic mediation of individual responses to environmental shocks.

Almost three decades earlier, Nei (1972) developed a concept of genetic distance, which was the difference in gene makeup across populations and geographies. Homogenous populations with less migration tend to have closer genetic distance than those with more integrations across races and countries. He begins with Malecot's coefficient of kinship and develops the concept of the rate of genetic substitution

---

31 McGrath et al. (2021); Young and McGrath (2020).

(which then determines genetic distance).[32] Eugenio Proto and Andrew Oswald (2017) then took that concept one step further and explored the extent to which it accounted for differences in well-being across populations and nations.

They began with Nei's measure of genetic distance between countries' populations and found that it correlated with international well-being differences. The correlation was not explained by potential omitted variables, such as prosperity, culture, or religion—the sort of confounding variables that geneticists refer to as the "chopsticks problem." They then looked at evidence that identifies the statistically significant (although controversial) relationship between the length variation in the 5-HTTLPR serotonin-transporter gene-linked polymorphism and mental well-being. They show how that varies across communities, populations, and individuals, positing that the spillover effects are larger than the individual effects. They also used the well-being levels of immigrants to explore the extent to which the well-being makeup of individuals who recently migrated to the United States is more closely related to their home country than the United States, finding convincing evidence to verify this.[33]

In the same vein, a recent paper by Kanazawa and Lopez (2021) explores how the outmigration of certain personality types helps explain why the Scandinavians are the happiest people on earth. For several centuries, the Vikings—who were notable for their shared traits with modern criminals: low agreeableness and conscientiousness and high levels of neuroticism—left Scandinavia for other countries to pillage, plunder, and rape and did not return. Many of those who survived eventually settled in what is today's Russia, which is one of the least happy of the world's wealthy countries. They posit that these trends in migration were large enough as a

32 Malecot (1959).
33 See also Ashraf and Galor (2013).

proportion of the respective populations and long-lasting enough (as they continued for several centuries) to have enduring effects on the respective gene pools. While this is less of a comprehensive study than Oswald and Proto's, it is, at the least, suggestive.

Earlier work published in the *Proceedings of the National Academy of Sciences*, by Jan-Emmanuel De Neve and Oswald (2012), based on studies of identical twins raised apart, found that they carried the same balance of the same transmitter gene polymorphism and that it affected their later life outcomes (positively), regardless of where they grew up. An interesting and less-known part of that research, which appears in the supplementary materials and is directly relevant to the discussion of racial difference in hope, is that African Americans are the racial cohort with the highest levels of the 5-HTTLPR transporter polymorphism, while Caucasians have the lowest levels. Caspi's international research confirms that people of color have higher levels of this gene transporter than Caucasians as well (although, again, that is based on limited studies).

Finally, along the same lines, some recent work on personality traits by psychologists S. G. Young and Robert McGrath (2020) in the United States finds that primal beliefs—that you can trust others, that things will work out, that the world is ultimately a safe place—are quite different across races, with African Americans standing out as the group most likely to have positive views, with negative views more likely to be associated with conspiracy theories and related phenomenon.

While limited in scale, this research resonates with the differences we find in the above data but also affirms the important role that the brain—and the neuroscience that seeks to understand it—has in explaining human emotions and behavior, including economic behavior. In a 2018 article, Carlos Alos-Ferrer posits that neuroscience and economic research not only inform but reinforce each other. Relevant to this exploration, he notes the importance of thinking about how specific regions and functions of the brain are interconnected. These interconnections apply to the social aspects of the brain—the so-called social brain—that interact with the environment. That, in turn, plays an important role in emotional regulation and cognitive functioning (both of which are associated with well-being and ill-being). When these functions are overloaded or malfunction, the result is stress and/or depression. Children raised in orphanages, who tend to experience early social deprivation and stress, often display cognitive impairments such as lack of impulse or emotional control. Schizophrenia, meanwhile, cannot be explained by genes alone—the environment plays a role.

As such, neuroscientists have a lot to teach economists, while economists' new thinking about how decision-making is often influenced by genetic traits interacting with the environment may benefit neuroscientists' thinking about the interconnections of the different functions of the brain. In terms of economic decision-making, this also supports models that extend beyond the realm of the rational, utility-maximizing Homo economicus to Homo sapiens and bounded rationality, departures from self-interested behavior, strategic behavior, shared values, and institutions. It also is directly relevant to understanding patterns in well-being—and ill-being—across individuals and places.

Some novel and soon-to-be-published work on brain health and a four-factor happiness scale (SHS) by Kokuban, Nemoto, and Yamakawa (2022) posits that the regions of the brain involved in emotional regulation are also linked to resilience, which affects the puzzling but increasingly established U-shaped relationship between age and happiness.[34] While the general motor (GM) functions of the brain tend

---

34 See Blanchflower and Oswald (2008); Blanchflower and Graham (2021); Clark (2019); and Weiss et al. (2012).

to decrease with age, FA (fractional anisotropy) does not. FA is more closely correlated with happiness and emotional regulation (and the regions it operates in are more involved in stress and emotional regulation) and does not decrease with age.

All of this advances our understanding of subjective well-being and, in my view, the agentic properties that hope displays and how it affects human lives. The interaction between the brain and the environment and the role of genes relevant to emotional regulation and to subjective well-being are key to this dimension of human existence that is not yet well understood. As in the case of the relative importance of genes or the environment in determining IQ, while there is consensus that both matter, there is much less consensus on how much explanatory power each dimension has.

The High Costs of Lack of Hope

A major reason I decided to write this book was watching despair increase in America. Despair in American society is a barrier to reviving its labor markets and productivity; it jeopardizes well-being, health, longevity, families, communities, and national security. The COVID-19 pandemic was a fundamental shock, exacerbating an already growing problem of despair. How and why does one of the wealthiest countries in the world have such high levels of despair?

Before the pandemic, the United States boasted robust stock markets and record low levels of unemployment. Yet those numbers masked the roughly 20% of prime-aged men (aged twenty-five to fifty-four) who had permanently dropped out of the labor force (OLF)—i.e., they were neither employed nor searching for work.[35] From 2005 to 2019, an average of

---

35 Those individuals no longer looking for work for more than six months drop out of the unemployment rate calculation altogether.

seventy thousand Americans died annually from deaths of despair (premature self-imposed deaths due to suicide, drug overdoses, and alcohol and other poisonings), with the numbers increasing gradually over this period. These deaths are concentrated among less-than-college-educated middle-aged whites, with the OLF population disproportionately represented.[36] Low-income racial minorities are significantly more optimistic than white people and much less likely to die of these deaths.

Sadly, this changed in 2018–19 due to the spread of fentanyl use among urban Black men and due to the COVID-19 shock more generally.[37] There were also worrisome increases in suicides among Black, Hispanic, Asian, and Pacific Islander youth (aged fifteen to twenty-four) during those same years. These trends merit more attention going forward.[38] As such, while much attention has gone to the despair of the white working class, despair is a broader social problem, albeit with different causal mechanisms across different cohorts.[39] Indeed, the most recent CDC estimates for overdose deaths in 2020 show a 30% increase compared to 2019, reaching ninety-three thousand overdose deaths in 2020.[40]

36 Deaths in this mortality category over the past decade were significant enough to drive overall U.S. mortality upward, giving us the pre-COVID-19 distinction of being the only wealthy country in the world where mortality was going up rather than down. For trends across populations and their links with subjective well-being indicators, see Graham and Pinto (2019).

37 https://well-beingtrust.org/wp-content/uploads/2021/05/2021-PainInThe Nation-FINAL-May-12.pdf.

38 Ramchad et al. (2021).

39 See, for example, Joe et al. (2009).

40 See https://www.nytimes.com/interactive/2021/07/14/upshot/drug -overdose-deaths.html. Remarkably, this number is close to the total predicted by Graham and team, based on EMS first responder data on overdose calls much earlier and in 2021. See "America's Crisis of Despair: A Federal Task Force for Economic Recovery and Societal Well-Being": https://www.brookings.edu /research/americas-crisis-of-despair-a-federal-task-force-for-economic-recovery -and-societal-well-being/.

Despair among the white working class reflects the negative effects of several waves of manufacturing decline. In contrast, minorities have made gradual, if difficult, progress in narrowing education and longevity gaps, and their high levels of hope and resilience have played an important role during this period. White despair contributes to decreasing levels of geographic mobility,[41] it reflects in our cognitive skill "deserts,"[42] and it has political spillovers. For example, counties with more respondents reporting lost hope before 2016 were more likely to vote for Donald Trump.[43] White males OLF, middle-class whites with high levels of debt, and whites from towns with high levels of fear of being "replaced" by growing minority populations were disproportionately represented among the individuals who stormed the U.S. Capitol on January 6.[44]

More generally, a wide body of evidence shows the long-term costs of prolonged unemployment on mental health. Indeed, it is one of the few life events that people do *not* adapt back from—meaning they do not return to their pre-event well-being levels over time, even though they adapt to many others, such as divorce or income changes. There are also spillover effects to the spouses of the long-term unemployed, which can lead to relationship breakdown and poor parental mental health. The latter, in turn, particularly for mothers, has negative effects on children's outcomes that extend into later adulthood.[45]

The prohibitive costs of health care in the United States—and the links between employment status and health insurance—make the cost of "failure" particularly high. Lack of hope,

---

41 Graham and Pinto (2020).

42 Hoxby (2021).

43 Herrin et al. (2018); Pinto et al. (2020).

44 Edsall (2021a); Feuer (2021).

45 See https://whatworkswell-being.org/resources/origins-of-happiness-briefing/.

defined here as the will to live and the possession of aspirations for the future, is a key factor. Despair describes the plight of the many who are ambivalent about whether they live or die. The latter impacts risk-taking, as in behaviors that jeopardize health and longevity. Entire communities can experience this helplessness, especially when confronted with difficult choices and change. They are often stuck in two worlds, with the old ways that held some meaning disappearing, while the changes needed to succeed in the new one seeming impossible in the absence of support. Death (slow or fast) becomes the simplest choice to stop the pain. Drug use and suicide are internal expressions of this, while expressed misery, frustration, and anger—which have security implications when widespread—are external ones.[46]

Another sign of despair, which has increased over the past decade and seems to be linked to our crisis of mental health, is the rising level of reported pain in the United States. More Americans report experiencing pain the previous day than respondents in thirty other countries, many of them in far less wealthy places.[47] Reported pain in the United States is also highest among the middle-aged rather than among the elderly, a departure from most other countries and historical patterns and likely a cohort effect, given the low state of well-being among the less-than-college-educated middle-aged whites in the United States today. Respondents of other races—particularly African Americans—have much lower levels of reported pain than whites.[48] As such, the increases in pain seem to mirror the trends driving our crisis of despair—or are part of it.

A related trend, which is unique to wealthy countries, is that pain reports are now highest among unemployed peo-

46 See https://whatworkswell-being.org/blog/happy-people-wear-seat-belts-risk-taking-and-well-being/.

47 Blanchflower and Oswald (2019).

48 Case, Deaton, and Stone (2021); Graham and Pinto (2019).

ple rather than employed workers.[49] This likely reflects the scarcity and declining quality and returns of blue-collar jobs, particularly in the United States. While despair is clearly a marker of the U.S. working class today, it also affects workers worldwide who are not prepared to navigate rapidly changing labor markets and skill requirements. Each of these trends is suggestive of psychological and physical pain.

We still do not know all the answers. As the authors of the well-known Copeland Study note, while despair may be a risk factor for diseases, it is also the end point of a process in which hope is lost.

> The public health successes of the 20th century have consistently allowed children to live longer than their parents. It is precisely because this recent pattern deviates from a century of progress that it has captured the attention of the public and the scientific community. This study takes a step toward understanding how a psychological state could derail the seemingly inexorable progress of modern medicine. However, this study is only one step, and additional work is needed to understand the origins of despair and premature mortality within individuals, families, and communities and how we can intervene to recover hope and forestall further morbidity and mortality.[50]

The Neuroscience of Despair

Neuroscientists note that despair is part of a complex contagion process that underlies the spread of far-right radicalization in the United States.[51] The confluence of online and physical organizing—including social media usage—enhances

---

49 Machia and Oswald (2021); Blanchflower and Bryson (2021).
50 Copeland et al. (2020).
51 Youngblood (2020).

the spread of radicalization and reinforces its transmission. Factors that underpin despair can make people more susceptible to extremist ideologies and create entire geographies that are prone to radicalization and violence. Indeed, poverty, unemployment, income inequality, and education levels are all relevant factors in radicalization, extremism, and mass shootings.[52]

Social identity and psychology, sacred values, neurocognitive deficits, emotions, and dehumanization are internal factors that can activate or inhibit radicalization and violent action. External factors include environment, culture, radical social networks, demographics, perceived grievances, traumatic life experiences, and social media (including both real and fake actors, as discussed above).[53] Increasingly, despair is considered a national security issue as well as a human welfare crisis in the United States. The increasing and seemingly "acceptable" (among some cohorts) attempts to override the democratic process in the past several years are part and parcel of this process.[54]

Conclusion and Next Steps

This chapter has brought a great deal of evidence—some novel and controversial—on the role of hope or lack thereof in charting the course of our futures. While lack of hope—

---

52 Piazza (2015); Medina et al. (2018).

53 Related to this, Professor Kenneth Thompson—based on his experience at the Substance Abuse and Mental Health Services Administration—highlights another factor in radicalization: the vulnerability of disaffected youths who have experienced events that shamed them and/or their families. Professor Thompson is an active participant in the Brookings Taskforce on Despair and Economic Recovery and is president of the Pennsylvania Psychiatric Council and also active in the Pittsburgh-Glasgow project on recovery.

54 Indeed, the Russians and Chinese were aware of these trends and took advantage of them in the manipulation of the 2016 presidential election. See Brookings Task Force on Despair and Economic Recovery, contribution made by task force member Fiona Hill, Brookings senior fellow.

ranging from despair to related or more acute mental health issues—was a problem for a forgotten few, it has now become a social crisis.

In part this is because of the challenges—as well as benefits—that technology-driven growth brings to countries everywhere. It is also because the land of opportunity is increasingly a winner-take-all society, with little help or empathy for those who fall behind.[55] Our social welfare and health systems, for example, are more fragmented than those of any other rich countries. While you can get the best health care in the world in the United States—if you can afford it— you can also get some of the worst. And if you lose your job or fall behind, your future is—at best—completely uncertain. Navigating the system without the assets and advantages of the rich is a difficult challenge; navigating the system without hope (or incredibly good luck) is near impossible.

Those who were most likely to get ahead or do better in the past, native whites, lacked the coping skills and the communities of empathy that those who were discriminated against or began as outsiders had to build to survive. As a result, minorities are more likely to still believe in the American Dream—or some form of it—than those who most believed in it previously and have now fallen behind (but remain skeptical of the government or other kinds of collective support). They lack a narrative—and the skills—for navigating current waters, both education and skill-wise. There are, of course, other issues at play, such as the complex dynamics underlying hope and resilience, including the interaction between genes and the environment that we do not fully understand, and now the political radicalization and division that is resulting from these problems.

There is no magic bullet and I do not claim to have any in this book. But I do believe that if we do not rebuild hope among

55 See, for example, Reeves (2018).

the next generation in populations and places where it has been lost, we will become a permanently divided society without a sustainable path to the future. In what follows, I present some novel evidence of what we know about the determinants and consequences of hope among deprived youths, and what we may learn from those who have lost it.

The following two chapters of the book, based on my surveys of young, low-income adolescents, provide some examples of the channels through which hope makes a difference to long-term outcomes, which include the importance of psychological support for goal achievement, particularly among those with less means and with less information about available opportunities and the tools necessary to achieve their goals. They also provide some sad examples of the downsides of lack of hope. Chapter 5 provides examples from research on well-being and the interventions it has led to, which promise to restore hope among populations and places where it has been lost. The last chapter raises some unanswered questions, both promising and difficult ones.

CHAPTER 3

Do Hope and Aspirations Lead to Better Outcomes?

EVIDENCE FROM A LONGITUDINAL SURVEY OF ADOLESCENTS IN PERU

As part of the effort to better understand hope and its causal properties, we interviewed poor young adults in Peru and the United States during the critical years when they had finished high school but were still deciding on their investments in education and in their futures in general.[1] We initially designed and fielded two rounds of the survey in Peru and then replicated it (adapted for a U.S. context) in low-income white and African American neighborhoods. What stands out in our research is the high levels of hope and aspirations of the respondents in Peru and of the minority respondents in the United States compared to the low hope, aspirations, and levels of trust among the white young adults. The objective was to explore the association between hope and related aspirations and future-oriented behavior. We designed the survey and the specific measures therein based on our interest in the outcomes that hope—combined with agency—lead to.

Our Peru study was distinct from existing ones in that we explicitly collected data on the focused aspirations and the personality traits of our respondents at two points in time, with the objective of understanding the interactions between

---

[1] This chapter draws heavily on Graham and Ruiz-Pozuelo (2022), forthcoming in the *Journal of Population Economics*.

them. (We have only collected one round of data at this point in the U.S. surveys, which are discussed in chapter 4.) While we see aspirations as focused on specific goals, we also see aspirations as integrally linked to hope and its implicit connection to the pursuit of a better life in the future. As such, our survey includes several questions that reflect the domains of the Big Five personality traits, as well as other questions that are tailored for adolescents at a point in their lives when they are making critical decisions about their futures. To our knowledge, this is one of the few surveys of its kind, with the benefits and risks that come with exploratory data.

We explored the link between aspirations and individuals' propensity to invest in the future, with four related objectives. First, we aimed to explore educational aspirations (and how they compare to occupational and migratory ones) among participants and to understand how aspirations vary with individual characteristics, childhood experiences, and the characteristics of the household in which they grew up. Second, the longitudinal nature of the study allowed us to examine how aspirations change over time *within* individuals. When possible, we determine whether adolescents met their aspirations or whether they mispredicted their futures. Third, we examined the link between aspirations and broad personality traits such as self-efficacy, subjective well-being, and locus of control. Lastly, we explored whether high aspirations are correlated with better human capital outcomes. We investigated this by looking at an individual's propensity to invest in their own future, as measured by education outcomes, time use, and engagement in risky behaviors such as substance use and delinquency.

Adolescence is a period of exploration in which individuals start to develop their self-identity and make important decisions about their future, ranging from education, relationships, entrance into the labor market, and health behaviors.[2] Risky behaviors such as unsafe sex, binge drinking, and delinquency tend to emerge during this period, potentially jeopardizing those plans.[3] Poor self-concepts (such as esteem) and hopelessness are also significant risk factors for adverse health behaviors during adolescence and adulthood.[4] Although aspirations are at the heart of many behaviors as well as a subject of interest in behavioral sciences, we know little about how aspirations shape those behaviors and subsequent accomplishments. Better understanding this relationship is particularly important for adolescents, who are at a point in their lives when aspirations will likely guide their choices about the future.

It is also possible that high aspirations can result in frustration if the goals are unattainable. A study based on the Young Lives panel study for India finds an inverse U-curve in the relationship between aspirations (of parents and adolescents) and education outcomes, with both low and overly high aspirations leading to worse outcomes than those in the "bell" of the curve (Ross 2019). Consistent with this result, another study finds that aspirations that are ahead—but not too far ahead (attainable in a shorter time frame)—provide the best incentives for key investments. The availability of opportunities and the social and circumstantial factors shaping aspirations, meanwhile, can hinder the aspirations of disadvantaged groups.[5]

This research also focuses on an understudied and significantly disadvantaged population group. Most of the evidence exploring the association between aspiration and human capital outcomes among adolescents comes from studies

2 Sawyer et al. (2012).
3 Pozuelo et al. (2021); Steinberg (2004).
4 Mann (2004).
5 See Ross (2019); Ray (2006); and Fruttero et al. (2021).

conducted in high-income countries.[6] Evidence from low- and middle-income countries, where 90% of the world's adolescents live and where far fewer resources and support systems are available, remains scarce. This study contributes to closing this gap.

Our results show that aspirations can be high among relatively poor individuals, and such aspirations are also resilient to a range of negative shocks in an already challenging context. Indeed, we find that aspirations are quite stable over time, which is particularly notable given that our respondents are in a period in which young lives change and develop. Aspirations in our sample are positively correlated with personality traits such as self-efficacy and subjective well-being, which helps explain their persistence. Finally, we find that high aspirations are strongly correlated with positive human capital outcomes such as higher investments in education and risk avoidance.

Aspirations and Their Determinants

Aspirations are commonly defined as a hope or ambition of achieving something. The concept of aspirations spans multiple—often interrelated—dimensions, both at the individual level (for example, the level of education toward which one aspires, type of job, fertility, and status) and at the collective level. The concept is different from expectations, which typically encompass an individual's beliefs about what they think they can achieve with effort—the most likely or realistic outcome.[7] While aspirations are aimed at specific goals—such as higher levels of education—these can also be a means to achieve higher and less well-defined

---

6 Beal and Crockett (2010); Mahler et al. (2017); Schmid et al. (2011); and Lerner (1982).

7 Dalton et al. (2016).

goals, such as having a better life (the loftier goals that hope leads to).

More formally, aspirations have three distinctive aspects. They are future-oriented, as they involve goals to be accomplished in the future. They act as motivators and drivers of effort, as they allow us to narrow our effort and attention toward accomplishing our goals and away from less relevant activities. Finally, they require some amount of effort to achieve.[8]

Aspirations evolve over time, as they are shaped by individual characteristics and one's personal experiences, families, and interactions with the social environment. Aspirations may also interact with objective factors such as capability and talent, leading to virtuous—or vicious—circles. As a result, several factors have been identified as potential determinants of aspirations, as well as possible interactions among these factors. The perspective of many behavioral economists is that aspirations are drawn from an individual's past experiences and, at the same time, are profoundly affected by one's social environment.[9] According to this view, individuals adjust their aspirations to what is perceived to be possible.

This view has implications for people living in poverty, as the lack of opportunity and/or information about what is possible can result in the following: a reduced "capacity to aspire"; frustration if the aspired goals are unattainable; and vicious cycles of continually lowering aspirations in ways that perpetuate poverty. This adaptation may be explained in part as a psychological preservation mechanism for those with limited capabilities or who live in conditions that do not allow them to aspire, as in the case of women in situations with unequal gender rights.[10]

8 Bernard and Taffese (2012).

9 Genicot and Ray (2017).

10 Appadurai (2004); Dalton et al. (2016); Frederick and Loewenstein (1999); Graham (2011, 2009); and Ray (2016).

Very poor people in difficult conditions may often report to be "happy"—in the sense of momentary contentment—but they typically score lower on evaluative questions that prime them to think about their lives as a whole. A more recent literature, meanwhile, focuses on optimism (as opposed to focused aspirations) and finds that some cohorts who lived in deprived conditions are much more optimistic than their counterparts of the same income levels. The optimistic ones tend to do better over time in the education and health arenas. This is the case, for example, for low-income African Americans and Hispanics compared to low-income whites in the United States.[11]

A second perspective is offered by personality and social psychologists (and some economists), who believe that aspirations are linked to but distinct from broad personality traits such as self-esteem, locus of control, and self-efficacy. Studies have shown that compared to measures of fluid intelligence such as IQ, personality traits are more likely to evolve over time and to interact with the environment well into middle age.[12] These personality traits, in turn, are known to predict future outcomes (such as education attainment and health and labor situations) as strongly as measures of cognitive ability.[13]

As noted in chapter 2, we consider aspirations as fitting into the broader concept of traits used by Heckman and Kautz (2012). They use the term "personality traits" to describe the attributes that are not captured by measures of abstract reasoning power. These attributes have many names, including soft skills, personality traits, noncognitive skills, character, and socioemotional skills. These different names connote different properties. The term "traits" suggests a sense of permanence and possibly also of heritability, while the terms "skills" and "character" suggest they can be learned. Their

11 Graham (2009); Graham and Pinto (2019).
12 Almlund et al. (2011); Bandura et al. (2001); and Dercon and Singh (2013).
13 Borghans et al. (2008); Heckman and Kautz (2012).

empirical work suggests that both cognitive and personality traits can change and be changed over the life cycle but through different mechanisms and at different ages.

Heckman and Kautz note, though, that most studies of the role of personality traits in determining outcomes, by both psychologists and economists, neglect to include the role of a deeper set of preferences or goals, which can also be thought of as traits. Achieving such goals requires certain traits, such as intelligence or conscientiousness. Under this view, traits are developed through practice, investment, and habituation, which are influenced by incentives. The apparent stability of expressed traits across situations may be a consequence of the stability of the goals and incentives themselves. Studies that account for the endogeneity of investments provide further evidence of the causal effect of education and cognitive and personality traits on outcomes. As such, human capital outcomes are at least in part endogenous to personality traits.

Heckman and Kautz rely on the so-called Big Five personality traits: conscientiousness, agreeableness, openness to experience, extroversion, and neuroticism/emotional stability. While these are largely stable over the life course, they can be influenced by experiences and parenting. The traits that we use in our survey—such as optimism, self-esteem, belief in hard work, mental states, impatience, and ability to make friendships—have many elements of these five traits. We chose our specific measures based on our interest in exploring the role of hope combined with agency as core features of aspirations. Our selection of personality trait measures was also influenced by whether they had already been tested in psychological studies of adolescents. As such, we built from the preexisting research on personality traits and outcomes but also adapted our metrics to our key questions of inquiry and to the population under study. Given that we focus on adolescents, relations with parents and/or peers are likely critical in forming preferences and incentives.

Methods

Study Context

We collaborated with the Instituto de Investigación Nutricional (IIN) in Lima, directed at the time by Dr. Mary Penny, to conduct a panel survey of four hundred adolescents in the district of San Juan de Lurigancho. The first study wave was conducted between May–June 2017, when the adolescents were aged eighteen and nineteen, and was followed by another subsequent wave of data in February 2020, with the interviews being completed just before the COVID-19 pandemic hit Peru. Institutional Review Board approval for this study was obtained before each round of data collection from the IIN.

San Juan de Lurigancho is a large peri-urban and relatively poor neighborhood of Lima with a population of over one million residing in a fifty-square-mile area. The district is home to several slums and to high levels of crime and youth unemployment.[14] The adolescents from our survey come from poor or near-poor families. Living standards range from concrete houses with newly acquired electricity and piped water and sewage, as well as access to metro and bus transport, to significantly more impoverished prefabricated homes farther away from the center and still in the process of acquiring these amenities.

As noted above, we focused on late adolescence (eighteen to nineteen years at Wave 1), as they have enough education and experience to observe while also being at a critical juncture in making vital choices. Most of them (83%) had completed secondary education in Wave 1 and were making decisions about their continued education, entrance into the labor market, family formation, and risky behaviors such as sexual relationships and substance use.

In the past decades, the Peruvian educational system has undergone significant transformation, leading to substan-

---

14 Andrade-Chaico and Andrade-Arenas (2019).

tive progress in providing access to education,[15] improved teacher-training programs, and increased education spending. While there has been progress, challenges remain—such as significant differences in access to and quality of education across rural and urban areas—and continue to show up in the performance statistics.

As in many other places around the world, returns to different levels of education are changing. In Peru, between 1980 and 2004, returns to primary, secondary, and technical education declined relative to returns to tertiary education. While returns to secondary education halved (from 12.6% to 6.3%) in that period, returns to tertiary doubled, reaching 17.3% by 2004.[16] The aspirations that our respondents have for college and postcollege education suggest they are aware of these differential returns.

While the parents of our San Juan de Lurigancho respondents do not have college educations and are in low-skill jobs— such as construction workers, taxi drivers, domestic servants, and local market owners—the aspirations of their children suggest a strong awareness of the need to get tertiary education to do better than their parents. Informal interviews in the area, meanwhile, suggest that parents play a strong role in this by encouraging them to seek higher education.[17]

Measures

ASPIRATIONS

We asked about aspirations in three domains: education (our primary variable of interest), occupation, and migration. Respondents were asked directly about their aspirations in both

---

15 In 2018, net enrollment rates were over 95% for primary education and 89.3% for secondary education. Gross enrollment ratio for tertiary education in 2017 was 70.7% (UNESCO 2018).

16 Yamada (2006).

17 In addition to informal interviews, one of the authors also received a number of comments supporting this pattern when presenting the first-round results at the IIN in November 2018.

waves. This approach has been shown to elicit more reliable measurements of individuals' aspirations when compared to indirect approaches that use other measures such as the self-reported minimum income needed to infer measures of aspirations.[18]

We first asked participants what level of education they would like to complete. The variable is coded on a four-point scale, where zero corresponds to low aspirations and three represents very high aspirations (postgraduate education). We then asked participants about the type of job or occupation they would like to achieve in life. We used the International Labour Organization's International Standard Classification of Occupations (ISCO-08) to rank our respondents' occupational aspirations. Scores range from zero (elementary occupations) to eight (managerial occupations). Finally, we asked adolescents whether they would like to migrate somewhere and, if they did, where. The variable is coded on an eight-point scale, where the score indicates how much a respondent aspires to migrate (zero = no desire to migrate, seven = aspires to migrate abroad).

PERSONALITY TRAITS

Emotional symptoms. These are measured using the five-item subscale of the Strengths and Difficulties Questionnaire (SDQ), one of the most widely used screening instruments to measure internalizing problems among young people.[19] The scale assesses symptoms such as headaches and stomachaches, worry, unhappy/tearful, nervous, and fears.

Locus of control. We selected four items on locus of control from Levenson's (1974) original scale. Two of these items measured internal locus of control while the others measured external (powerful others and chance) locus of control. All the

18 Bernard and Tafesse (2014).
19 Goodman (1997).

above items were measured on a Likert scale, from strongly disagree (= zero) to strongly agree (= three). The scale evaluates which forces individuals consider as determining their lives.

Self-efficacy. We used five items from Schwarzer and Jerusalem's (1995) Generalized Self-Efficacy Scale. For each item, participants could choose from "not at all true" (score = zero) to "exactly true" (score = three). The scores for each of the five items were summed to give a total score. This construct measures an individual's general confidence to cope with unforeseen or demanding situations.

Life satisfaction. This measure, which assesses current satisfaction with life, is based on responses to the best possible life (BPL) Cantril ladder question. This commonly used question asks respondents to place themselves on a nine-step ladder in which they compare their lives to the best possible life they can imagine.

We also measured respondents' beliefs that hard work will get them ahead, their willingness to take risks, and their sociability, self-esteem, and optimism. We measured impatience by administering the classic discount-rate question, where respondents decide between immediate sums of money today versus higher sums in the future.

Both our measures of locus of control and of impatience—and their strong association with our definition of aspirations—share similarities with Hofstede's (2001) concept of long-term orientation, which he saw as varying across both people and cultures. In contrast to Hofstede, we focus on differences in these traits within a homogenous population rather than differences across cultures. The works of Galor and Özak (2016) and Figlio et al. (2019), which focus on long-term outcomes in terms of risky behaviors, saving money, and education, are more directly related to our analysis and our measures of time preference and ability to delay gratification.

INDIVIDUAL AND HOUSEHOLD CHARACTERISTICS

Socioeconomic status. We measured respondents' socioeconomic statuses using a household asset index, which included several questions on housing quality, access to services, and ownership of consumer durables. We created a weighted average, where a higher wealth index indicates a higher socioeconomic status. We also collected data on six types of negative shocks: robbery; whether he/she suffered from an accident (defined as serious injuries that would prevent respondents from doing their normal activities and/or require medical attention); sickness of oneself or a family member or death of family member; whether one parent or both parents left the household; unemployment shock; or natural disaster. Finally, we included a battery of questions on education, health, family support, and employment.

HUMAN CAPITAL OUTCOMES

These included school outcomes, which were assessed by the highest level of education attained by our respondents and whether they are full-time students. We also asked respondents how much time they allocated to school-related tasks and whether they participated in any professional development training, such as language courses.

In a separate and self-administered section, we asked respondents about their sense of self-respect in their interactions with parents and peers; their usage of cigarettes and alcohol; their attitudes about risky sexual behaviors and delinquency and their proclivity to those. Answering these questions was optional, and respondents provided their answers to the interviewers in a sealed envelope.

Statistical Analysis

To explore whether high aspirations result in better future outcomes, we took a two-step approach.

In Model 1, we used a lagged, dynamic model to explore whether aspirations at Wave 1 correlated with future outcomes at Wave 2. We controlled for a range of individual-level and household-level characteristics, as well as personality traits.

In Model 2, we exploited the fact that we had a panel study to estimate an individual fixed effects model. The fixed effect model eliminated one major source of confounding effects by controlling for any unobserved time-invariant variables that may be correlated with the explanatory variables.[20] That is, in a fixed effects specification, constant variables (observed or unobserved) such as sex, parental education, and ethnicity were dropped out of the model, thus eliminating any concerns we might have had about their potential confounding effects. Although this model is not sufficient to claim any causal relation, it allows us to get a better identification of the relationship between aspirations and human capital outcomes while controlling for within-person traits.

While Model 2 may be more precise, Model 1 allowed us to explore the dynamics underlying the later-term outcomes of our adolescents. More information about each model, along with the model specifications, can be found in the appendix.

Results

Basic Sociodemographics and Attrition Analysis

Table 3.1 shows the main descriptive statistics across both waves of data. Mean average age is eighteen years old at Wave 1, with the sample evenly split between males and females. Levels of education are relatively high, with only 3% of the sample having no formal education in Wave 1. By Wave 2, more respondents had married, had children, and lost a parent. Average years of education increased, but so

---

20 Woolridge (2010).

Table 3.1. Basic Sociodemographics

	Wave 1 (n = 400)	Wave 2 (n = 301)	t-statistic	p-value
Female	53.8%	57%	−0.98	0.33
Age of child (in years)	18	21	−57.18	0.00***
Married	4.8%	17%	−4.95	0.00***
Any children	13.0%	19.9%	−2.12	0.03*
Deceased parent	8.3%	13%	−2.04	0.04*
Attained primary	97.3%	99%	−1.75	0.08
Attained secondary	82.8%	94%	−4.64	0.00***
Enrolled in school	68.0%	50%	4.75	0.00***
Average years of education	11.8	14.3	−15.20	0.00***
Worked in the past 12 months	76.5%	79%	−0.92	0.36
Currently employed	35.3%	58%	−6.06	0.00***
Subjective relative income (0–6 score)	3.0	3.0	−0.4	0.73
Average number of negative shocks experienced	2.3	1.3	10.36	0.00***

Note: All variables except age, average years of education, subjective relative income, and average number of negative shocks experienced are dummy variables. P-value of difference between the two waves is from two-tailed t-test. The stars represent statistical significance as follows: * $p < 0.05$, ** $p < 0.01$, *** $p < 0.001$.

did the number of adolescents who dropped out of school. Overall, half of the sample was no longer enrolled full-time in education at Wave 2. Respondents reported that the main reason for leaving school was lack of financial resources (for example, respondents could not afford school and had to look for a job). Most respondents (90.5%) experienced some form of negative shock. The most common shocks were thievery, followed by a parent leaving the household, an accident, and a family sickness.

In terms of household-level characteristics, and according to data from the wealth asset index, most of the houses have access to electricity, water, and a toilet. Further, over 95% of households have access to a TV and a phone, 87% to a fridge, and 60% to a computer in the house. Many of their parents had not completed higher than secondary levels of education. As noted above, most of the fathers were construction workers, informal sector merchants, bus or taxi drivers, or carpenters, while most mothers were housekeepers, merchants/street vendors, seamstresses, or housecleaners.

Ninety-nine adolescents fell out of the survey at follow-up, resulting in an attrition rate of 24.75%. (Please see table A1 in the appendix in the original article [Graham and Ruiz-Pozuelo 2002], which shows attrition bias across observables.) On average, males and adolescents who were not enrolled full-time at Wave 1 were more likely to drop out at follow-up. Educational aspirations were slightly lower among those who were lost to follow-up. We observed no differences in occupational aspirations, aspirations to migrate, or other covariates such as personality traits or risky behavior measures. Studies of attrition rates in panels cite factors such as unhealthy lifestyles or psychological distress as common predictors, but those do not seem to be at play in this instance.

We have reasons for attrition for most of these individuals (75%). This is rare, as most studies lack good data on reasons for attrition. In our case, our survey team was diligent in seeking out reasons for missing respondents and were often able to get information about why they had moved away from their friends or family. Half of the missing sample had moved to a different location (within Peru and/or abroad to countries such as Spain or the United States). The rest were either not available (12%), traveling (5%), or working (4%) at the time of the interview. Parents refused to allow participation in the survey in three cases, and one adolescent had a high-risk pregnancy and could not participate. Given that a significant percent of the attrition group traveled abroad to seek better jobs, we cannot attribute attrition to low aspirations or worse performance.

In peri-urban neighborhoods such as this one in Peru it is quite common for young adults to move elsewhere to look for better jobs or other opportunities. In our case, those respondents with slightly higher education aspirations were less likely to leave the neighborhood, likely because they were enrolled in their continuing education. More generally, attrition rates for panels greatly vary. The Rand American Life Panel, for example, has a low rate of 15%, while, across studies more generally, the range is 30–70%.[21] As such, our attrition rate of 25% for a panel of young respondents living in a relatively unstable economic context is on the low end.

What Do Adolescents Aspire to Do in the Future?

We find remarkably high aspirations in Wave 1. Overall, 41% of our sample report wanting to achieve postgraduate education (master's or doctoral degrees) with 47% aiming for university and 10% aspiring to technical education. Occupational aspirations are also high, with most respondents aspiring to high-skilled professional jobs. Almost all respondents (93%) aspire to migrate, with half of those wanting to migrate to another district within the same province, and a quarter to a distant country (figures A1–A3 in the appendix).

The main reasons for wanting to migrate are to find better education and employment opportunities or to escape high levels of crime and delinquency. We find a positive correlation across all three types of aspirations (educational, occupational, and migratory). When asked a follow-up question about whether they can achieve their desired level of education and occupation, 89% and 96% of the sample responded affirmatively, respectively. Figure 3.1 shows how aspirations change depending on individual-level and household-level characteristics. To construct this figure, we rescaled the three types of aspirations on a ten-point scale to allow for comparisons across and within types of aspirations. First,

---

21 Gustavson et al. (2012).

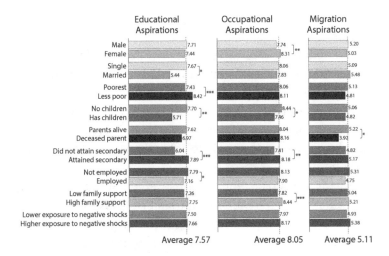

Figure 3.1. Aspirations by subgroups. *Note*: Data from Wave 1 were used to construct this figure. We rescaled the three types of aspirations on a ten-point scale to make it easier to compare the average level of aspirations across all three types. All individual characteristics are dummy variables. The stars represent statistical significance as follows: * p < 0.05, ** p < 0.01, *** p < 0.001.

occupational aspirations are significantly higher than educational and migration aspirations (i.e., the average level of occupational aspirations is 8.05, while it is 7.57 for the educational aspirations), and this difference is statistically significant at 0.01 level.

There is also some heterogeneity in aspirations depending on individual characteristics. For example, we find lower educational aspirations among adolescents who were married and those who had a child. This is not a surprise given that those who marry or have a child at a young age have likely reduced their possibilities to continue education. We also find that educational aspirations are lower among the poor. For example, 38% of respondents from poor households aspire to achieve postgraduate education, compared to 56% of respondents from highest income households, which are, at most, aspiring lower middle-class. Educational aspirations are also lower among those respondents who did not attain secondary education and were employed—presumably because they had to skip school or stop education all together.

Occupational aspirations, meanwhile, are higher for females, those who had attained secondary education, did not have a child, and for those who lived in a household with high levels of family support. Lastly, aspirations to migrate are lower for those adolescents who lost a parent, likely because they had to stay home to help take care of other family members.

Finally, we find no difference in levels of aspirations among individuals who were highly exposed to negative shocks compared to those who were not. This is likely because negative shocks like robbery or accidents are common in neighborhoods such as San Juan de Lurigancho, making it more likely that people adapt to them. It is also at least suggestive of resilience—acquired by living in difficult circumstances—as a driving channel of the persistence of aspirations despite the obstacles.

Do Aspirations Change over Time?

Aspirations may change due to new experiences, past achievements and failures, and interactions with the social and academic environment. With time, individuals obtain a better understanding of the world and what is possible and, especially during adolescence, start to realign their behavior with the social norms of those they identify with and/or with difficult realities in their situations.[22] And, as noted above, personality can evolve over time due to experience and changing preferences. At the same time, if aspirations and related goals are shaped by strong preferences and incentives, they are more likely to persist over time, as Heckman and Kautz observe.

---

22 Gottfredson (2002); Sebastian et al. (2008).

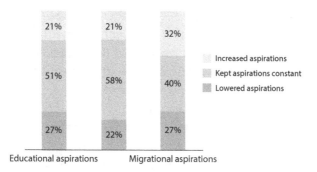

Figure 3.2. Changes in aspirations *within* individuals over time

In the first wave of data, our respondents were aged eighteen to nineteen years old, at which point they likely had enough education and life experiences to internalize personal and contextual barriers to attaining these aspirations (aspirations and expectations converge). Indeed, we find that education aspirations remain relatively stable over time (table A2 in the appendix). We calculated t-test for differences in average aspirations across both waves and failed to reject the null hypothesis that these two were different (p = 0.09). This pattern was also consistent with occupational aspirations (p = 0.7) and aspirations to migrate (p = 0.8). Half of the sample kept their aspirations constant, and the rest of the sample was evenly split between those who increased and decreased their aspirations (figure 3.2).

Do Optimists Mispredict Their Futures?

An obvious question in this narrative is whether optimists succeed in their aspirations or mispredict their futures. Misprediction could lead to frustration and worse outcomes in the long run. Alternatively, it might simply result in no change in well-being among innately optimistic respondents, who remain optimistic regardless of shocks or setbacks.

We are not able to measure whether aspirations were met for most of our sample since we do not observe the complete education or labor market trajectories. Respondents are twenty to twenty-two years old at Wave 2, and a third of them are still attending university. Only four of our respondents had completed university at the time of Wave 2 (all of whom had aspired to attain that goal at Wave 1). For those enrolled in university, we can only conclude they are on track to meet their aspirations but cannot say anything about their final outcomes.

Among the individuals with lower educational aspirations who might have had time to achieve those, we observe that those individuals who aspired to technical school (n = 39) in Wave 1, met their aspirations at Wave 2. While the sample sizes are small, these results suggest that the aspirations that adolescents set for themselves are realistic.

Are Aspirations and Personality Traits Correlated?

How high an individual aspires is determined by their own beliefs about what they think they can achieve as well as their personality traits. Typically, individuals evaluate their internal and/or external constraints (one's locus of control and/or credit) and exclude some of the unattainable options. Particularly for those living in poverty, this plays a crucial role since an individual's perceived returns are often inaccurate due to imperfect information.

Mean levels of character traits in our sample are high and continue to be so in Wave 2 (table A3 in the appendix). Respondents improve in internal locus of control, self-esteem, and optimism scores over time. They are also more likely to believe that hard work will get them ahead and are more willing to take risks. On average, life satisfaction scores are relatively high in both waves. Most respondents (79%) believe they were happier in Wave 1 than they were ten years ago, and

Table 3.2. Correlation across Types of Aspirations and Personality Traits

	Educational aspirations	Occupational aspirations	Aspirations to migrate
Emotional symptoms (0–10 score)	−0.04	0.04	0.07
Internal locus of control (0–6 score)	0.05	0.01	−0.02
External locus of control (0–6 score)	−0.06	0.01	0.06
Self-efficacy (0–15 score)	0.09*	0.04	0.05
Subjective well-being (0–8 score)	0.13***	0.01	0.03
Impatience	−0.11**	−0.09*	−0.04
Belief in hard work	0.12**	0.11**	0.08*
Willingness to take risks	−0.02	−0.08*	0.00
Sociability	0.01	0.04	−0.04
Self-esteem	0.04	0.04	0.04
Optimism	0.02	0.05	0.07

Note: The first five variables are scores, with the range shown in parentheses. The remaining traits are dummy variables. Pairwise correlations were calculated pooling data from both waves. The stars represent statistical significance as follows: * $p < 0.05$, ** $p < 0.01$, *** $p < 0.001$.

similarly, most (76%) believed they were happier in Wave 2 than they were in Wave 1. This is consistent with other work we have done exploring optimism levels over time, where we find that respondents who are optimistic in earlier periods tend to remain optimistic in later periods and to do better in the income and education realms, even if they have suffered some negative shocks along the way (Graham and Pinto 2019; O'Connor and Graham 2018). In table 3.2 we report the pairwise correlations between all three types of aspirations and personality traits. Educational aspirations are positively correlated with self-efficacy, subjective well-being, and belief in hard work, and are negatively correlated with impatience. Occupational aspirations are negatively correlated with impatience and willingness to take risks, and positively with belief in hard work. Aspirations to migrate are correlated with belief in hard work.

*Do High Aspirations Lead to Better Human
Capital Outcomes?*

To explore this question, we look at the correlation between aspirations and future outcomes, including education outcomes, time use, and an adolescent's engagement in risky behaviors such as substance use and delinquency. Most of our respondents experimented with alcohol, half of the sample smoked, and a third engaged in risky sex (table A4 in the appendix). Engagement in these behaviors increased over time/with age. Results from Model 1 (lagged model) are presented in table 3.3. To allow for comparisons, we report standardized coefficients and only show the parameter of interest for all three types of aspirations. Educational aspirations at Wave 1 predict better outcomes at Wave 2. Keeping other factors constant, a 1 standard deviation increase in educational aspirations at Wave 1 increases average years of education and enrollment status by 0.25 and 0.27 standard deviations. Similarly, it increases the share of time spent on school-related activities and professional development by 0.30 and 0.14 standard deviations. In contrast, a 1 standard deviation increase in educational aspirations at Wave 1 decreases the likelihood of smoking and engaging in unsafe sex by 0.14 and 0.19 standard deviations. Occupational aspirations at Wave 1 also predict better educational outcomes (effect sizes range from 0.12 to 0.16 standard deviations) and more time spent on school-related activities. Lastly, high aspirations to migrate are associated with more time allocated to professional development training and being less likely to carry a weapon.

To obtain a better identification of the relationship between aspirations and human capital outcomes, we specify an individual fixed effects model. The results are presented in table 3.4. In general, we find similar conclusions to those found in Model 1, particularly for educational aspirations. Specifically, an increase in educational aspirations by 1 standard deviation predicts an

Table 3.3. Model 1—Lagged Model: Aspirations at Wave 1 on Outcomes at Wave 2

	Educational aspirations	Occupational aspirations	Migration aspirations
	Standardized β coefficients	Standardized β coefficients	Standardized β coefficients
Average years of education	0.25** (0.09)	0.12* (0.05)	0.04 (0.06)
Enrolled full-time	0.27*** (0.06)	0.12* (0.06)	0.03 (0.06)
Share of time spent on school-related activities	0.30*** (0.06)	0.16** (0.05)	0.02 (0.06)
Pursue any professional development activities	0.14* (0.07)	0.01 (0.06)	0.13* (0.06)
Smokes cigarettes	−0.14* (0.06)	−0.04 (0.05)	−0.05 (0.06)
Drinks alcohol	−0.03 (0.05)	−0.10 (0.06)	−0.07 (0.05)
Risky sex	−0.19** (0.07)	−0.11 (0.07)	−0.08 (0.07)
Carries weapon	0.03 (0.04)	0.02 (0.02)	−0.10* (0.05)

Note: Each row was a separate regression. We applied robust standard errors (in parentheses) and standardized the coefficients using the whole sample's standard deviation. Each regression controlled for the following individual- and household-level characteristics: sex, total shocks experienced, and a household asset index constructed from information on ownership of a range of durable goods, housing characteristics, sanitation, and access to services. We also controlled for the following personality traits: emotional symptoms, locus of control (internal and external), self-efficacy, subjective well-being, impatience, and belief in hard work. The stars represent statistical significance as follows: * $p < 0.05$, ** $p < 0.01$, *** $p < 0.001$.

increase in enrollment status and time spent on school activities by 0.26 and 0.21 standard deviations, respectively. These effect sizes are similar to those in Model 1. High educational aspirations are also predictive of avoiding carrying weapons, which was not a significant finding in the first model. Further, a 1 standard deviation increase in occupational aspirations reduces the likelihood of smoking by 0.18 standard deviation. The rest of the associations are not statistically significant.[23]

23 The full specifications for Model 1 and Model 2 can be found in tables A5 and A6 in the appendix of Graham and Pozuelo (2022), and figure A4 compares the coefficients from the lagged model (Model 1) and the correlations with fixed effects (Model 2) for educational aspirations.

Table 3.4. Model 2—Individual Fixed Effects Model

	Educational aspirations	Occupational aspirations	Migration aspirations
	Standardized β coefficients	Standardized β coefficients	Standardized β coefficients
Average years of education	0.08 (0.06)	0.01 (0.05)	0.02 (0.06)
Enrolled full-time	0.26*** (0.06)	0.08 (0.07)	0.05 (0.06)
Share of time spent on school-related activities	0.21*** (0.05)	0.03 (0.05)	0.02 (0.06)
Pursue any professional development activities	−0.07 (0.06)	−0.04 (0.06)	−0.04 (0.07)
Smokes cigarettes	−0.05 (0.06)	−0.18** (0.06)	0.11 (0.06)
Drinks alcohol	0.07 (0.06)	−0.07 (0.07)	0.10 (0.07)
Risky sex	−0.00 (0.07)	−0.02 (0.08)	0.10 (0.07)
Carries weapon	−0.14* (0.07)	−0.13 (0.07)	0.03 (0.06)

Note: Each row was a separate regression. We applied robust standard errors (in parentheses) and standardized the coefficients using the whole sample's standard deviation. Each regression controlled for the following individual- and household-level characteristics: marital status, employment status, and total shocks experienced. We also controlled for the following personality traits: emotional symptoms, locus of control (internal and external), self-efficacy, subjective well-being, impatience, and belief in hard work. The stars represent statistical significance as follows: * $p < 0.05$, ** $p < 0.01$, *** $p < 0.001$.

More generally, the fixed effects estimates show that the relationship between aspirations and human capital outcomes is robust to holding within-person traits constant. One reason for this, noted above, is that aspirations and other traits are endogenous to the goals and preferences that frame these traits and help explain their persistence. While intuitive, this also complicates the task of identifying clear channels of causality.

Conclusion

Our research attempted to shed light on the role of aspirations in generating better future outcomes. We conducted a panel study with adolescents (aged eighteen to nineteen years at

Wave 1) in a poor and near poor peri-urban neighborhood in Lima, Peru. We asked about aspirations in three domains: education, occupation, and migration, with a particular focus on education. We designed the specific measures therein based on our interest in exploring the role of hope—an understudied but important trait in our view—combined with agency as core features of aspirations and the outcomes they lead to. As such, our survey includes several questions tailored for adolescents at a point in their lives when they are making critical decisions about their futures. To our knowledge, our survey is one of a few of its kind, with the benefits and risks that come with such exploratory data.

Our main finding was remarkably high levels of aspirations among our survey population, with over 80% of our respondents aspiring to complete university or postgraduate education. Further, aspirations are sticky over time, with half the sample keeping their aspirations constant two years later (a quarter increased them). Lastly, high aspirations are associated with better future outcomes. Respondents with high aspirations in Wave 1 were more likely to have better educational and health-related outcomes as measured by school enrollment, time allocated to school activities and professional development, and lower engagement in risky behaviors such as substance use and risky sex in Wave 2. This supports our (and others') priors that individuals with high aspirations and/or hope for the future are more likely to invest in those futures and to avoid behaviors likely to jeopardize their futures.

Our study has some limitations. First, we looked at the association between aspirations and human capital outcomes using observational evidence; thus, this study does not claim any clear causal relation. To minimize potential endogeneity concerns, we controlled for a range of important confounders and specified a lagged model and a fixed effects model (which eliminates one major source of confounding by controlling for any unobserved time-invariant heterogeneity that may be correlated with the explanatory variables). Second, we relied on self-report measures to measure our outcomes, which could be affected by recall or reporting bias. Nevertheless, all sensitive questions (e.g., risky behaviors) were asked using a self-administered segment, which has been shown to reduce measurement error.[24]

Third, we were not able to measure whether aspirations were met for most of our sample since we did not observe the complete education or labor market trajectories. While we cannot say anything about their final human capital outcomes, our results suggest that most of our respondents are on track to meet their aspirations. Lastly, we do not have data on the respondents' peers and their aspirations. This is particularly important during adolescence, as adolescents spend more time with peers, place more value on what their peers think (and aspire to) than what their families think.[25]

We also cannot say anything about parental aspirations for their children. However, anecdotal data based on interviews with those who work in this neighborhood and in Lima more generally suggest that there is a strong shared belief in the importance of education among these parents—even though they do not have tertiary education—which provides a support system for the young adults in our sample. Indeed, 88% of our respondents report that their education is paid for by their parents. (We explore the role of parental aspirations explicitly in the Missouri surveys, with some surprising findings.)

While associational, our results suggest that aspirations may be an important lever to improve overall well-being and long-term outcomes. Recent evidence shows that it is possible to intervene to alter aspirations and that this may have a causal influence on a range of human capital outcomes. A study conducted in the Dominican Republic estimated that

---

24 Okamoto et al. (2002).
25 Blakemore and Mills (2014).

providing information on the returns to education (thus changing the perceived returns) increased completion of secondary education by 0.20–0.35 additional years. Using census data for Brazil, another study found that exposure to soap operas with strong female role models has a significant effect in lowering birth rates, with the strongest effect among women from lower socioeconomic status. Beaman et al. show that female leadership influences adolescent girls' career aspirations and educational attainment. Lastly, a study conducted in rural Ethiopia found that playing a documentary featuring role models led to higher aspirations and better saving and investment decisions among adults.[26]

The driving channel in all these cases—as well as in other experiments—seems to be the provision of a hope channel where one previously did not exist, as in the case of Haushofer and Fehr's study, cited in chapter 5. Their study showed that the provision of hope in very poor populations in Africa—via the gift of a cow or some other form of livestock—improved household outcomes the following year, with hope being the most important driver. While these studies cannot reveal how long the behavioral changes last, they are, at the least, suggestive of a virtuous circle.

In Peru, education levels are high enough to drive awareness of the increasing returns to higher versus secondary education, which is likely an important incentive factor. Yet our data also suggest that traits such as optimism, self-efficacy, and internal locus of control matter independently of that. Our results show that aspirations are persistent *within* respondents, with high aspirations remaining at the same levels over the two-year period for most respondents. While two years is not a long time-frame, it is typically a time of many changes for individuals in their late teens and early

---

26 La Ferrara et al. (2012); Beaman et al. (2012); Jenson (2010); and Bernard et al. (2014).

twenties, and it is striking that the aspirations of most were persistent throughout.

This certainly suggests that aspirations are not just fleeting traits, as the literature shows that strong preferences and incentives shaping goals help explain the persistence of such traits. The strong emphasis on educational achievement in Peru, meanwhile, likely plays a role in the persistence of aspirations in our sample. And, as noted above, we see aspirations as aimed at specific goals but also at the achievement of broader and less well-defined ones, such as seeking a better life. The specific goals are often a more tangible and achievable means to attain the higher ones, such as achieving a certain level of education, which, in turn, leads to a broader opportunity set.

There is much more we need to know, both about the drivers of aspirations and how the in-person and environmental factors interact in determining them, and about the consistency and durations of the channel from aspirations to better human capital outcomes. At this juncture, though, our findings suggest that hope and aspirations matter to actual outcomes and that they may be particularly important in the context of deprived populations. This is because they do not have the same level of financial support and other advantages as wealthier populations that facilitate making key investments in their own human capital. In the next chapter, I turn to the findings of a much smaller but similar survey we fielded among low-income adolescents in the United States.

CHAPTER 4

Different Visions of the Future among Low-Income Young Adults

CAN THE AMERICAN DREAM SURVIVE?

What determines hope and despair? This is a critical question for young adults making key investments—or not—in their futures. In the previous chapter we found surprisingly high aspirations for higher levels of education—and better futures—among low-income adolescents in Peru. Sadly, the same is not true for all the low-income young adult respondents in our surveys in the United States, particularly white young adults, who are, in general, not hopeful about their futures and lack aspirations to pursue higher education. How can this be in the land of opportunity, among the prevalent belief that hard work and education can get you ahead?

In contrast, we find consistency and persistence in high hopes and aspirations in Peru, as I describe in chapter 3. Eighty-five percent of our respondents aspired to attend university or even pursue graduate-level education; 95% of those thought they could meet their goals. And, at least as evidenced by a follow-up survey three years later, these aspirations were persistent, and most high-aspirations respondents were on track to meet their goals three years later. The aspirations seem to persist despite negative shocks (except to individuals' own health) and were usually supported by a mentor either in the family or in the community.

We conducted a similar survey among low-income adolescents in St. Louis, Missouri, with a focus on racial differences in hopes and beliefs in higher education. Most notable in our findings are the strong differences across races: only three of the African American or other minority adolescents reported little hope and no parental support for their aspirations, while only two of the white respondents reported *having* hope and parental support for their aspirations.

These differences are not accounted for by income or other material differences (the white respondents were, on average, wealthier, at least in terms of self-reported income) or by major differences in health or access to health insurance (the African American adolescents were less likely to have health insurance). And while African American adolescents were more likely to have had at least one parent with some college than white ones, they were also more likely to have had a parent either no longer living in the home or deceased.

Large cultural differences are seemingly at play. White respondents were more likely to have a strong individual locus of control and an ethos of individual effort, and they were far less likely to trust in others and in their neighbors. White families were more likely to own their homes than minority families, yet minorities remained more hopeful and more likely to want to pursue further education.

Accepting that this generalization is risky with such a small and in-depth survey, it seems that despite equivalent or greater obstacles in their paths, minorities are still more hopeful and more likely to invest in their ability to get ahead. In contrast, low-income whites are falling behind in income, education, and health status relative to their wealthier white peers; they are also being surpassed in some areas by the low-income minorities that they used to do better than in the past. And they do not believe their futures can be better. While these patterns appear in the large N data on differences across races in optimism and resilience, it is striking—and sobering—to see that these patterns are also consistent in the responses of the next generation.

The Thinking about the Future Survey in Missouri

Our Missouri survey efforts began in September 2019, as the Peru work wrapped up. After some initial usual delays, we faced major obstacles in fielding the survey due to the onset of COVID-19. We began with the support of two school district superintendents, Art McCoy of Jennings and Kevin Carl of Hancock (both with a reputation of dedication and raising the level of school quality in their long struggling districts), and the expertise and logistical support of NORC, the survey arm of the University of Chicago. Our original intent was to field the surveys via in-person interviews, with the NORC personnel supervising, in the community center of each school district.

The Jennings district is primarily an African American demographic and the Hancock district is largely white. There are some other minorities in both—one of our respondents is originally from Thailand, one is an Arab male who just moved to St. Louis from Kansas, and there are a few Hispanic respondents. In general, though, the demographic is evenly split between African Americans and whites and across district lines.

After postponing in-person interviews two times during the evolution of COVID-19, we resorted to a mail-in survey. The mail surveys were fielded initially in July 2021 and the last batch of response reminders was sent out in December 2021. As of this writing, thirty-two responses were received from the roughly one hundred and fifty students—aged eighteen to twenty and either about to graduate or just graduated from high school—we sent questionnaires to (we sent them to the 2020 graduates and the 2021 soon-to-be-graduates in each school district, using the address lists provided by the schools). We still hope to receive roughly ten more.

The questionnaire (appended at the end of the book) was a version of the Peru survey adapted for a U.S. context. It covered similar background questions, including respondents' living situations and relations with their parents; their financial, health, and education status; and their aspirations in terms of future education levels, employment, and migrating or moving to a place with more opportunities. We also asked a battery of questions about hope for the future, locus of control, self-esteem, and goal achievement, and information about risky behaviors such as smoking, drinking, and sexual behaviors.

Respondents who completed the surveys received a gift card worth twenty-five dollars in round 1 (July 2021) and forty dollars in the final round (December 2021). Our response rate—roughly 20%—was disappointing, but not considered low in today's survey research environment and not for a mail-in survey for a cohort that is typically unlikely to respond. Yet the respondents who did complete the survey gave what seemed to be honest and complete answers. Only one respondent failed to include her name and address and to fill out most of the questions on the questionnaire (as a result forfeiting her gift card).

Our respondents were primarily from St. Louis—only a few of them had moved in recent years from out of town/ state—and most lived in the same house for most of their lives. Almost all reported they would like to move—at least to another county—and at the same time said they did not have the skills and finances to do so, and that St. Louis is where their families were located. (It is worth nothing that people from St. Louis tend to stay there; they have a lower out-migration rate than similar-sized cities with roughly the same per capita income.)[1]

---

1 The out-migration rate for St. Louis from 2015–19 was thirty-two per one thousand residents, compared to Baltimore, where it was thirty-nine per one

Patterns in the Responses

Given the small sample size, it is impossible to conduct a robust econometric analysis of the survey results. Still, as noted above, there are remarkable regularities across responses, especially across races, as opposed to other demographic differences, regularities that reflect differential hopes and beliefs in education across low-income groups and are both surprisingly positive and sadly negative depending on which race they represent.

As noted above, African American respondents were more hopeful, more likely to trust others, and more likely to have a parent who supported their educational aspirations than white ones. The patterns were remarkably consistent. While the African American youths often had one parent missing, they were also more likely to have one parent who had at least some college education. The other minority respondents of the survey, with a few exceptions, tended to display the hopeful traits that the African American respondents displayed.

White respondents tended to have more consistent responses than minorities on locus of control and belief that their own individual work would get them ahead, while at the same time trusting those in their community less and having worse relations with their parents (in general, although there were exceptions). What is also remarkable is the extent to which the white respondents' parents did not support them in attaining education beyond a high school education. Only a few parents supported an additional year or two of technical or vocational education; only two out of roughly fifteen white respondents had parents who supported college completion

---

thousand residents; to Denver, where it was forty-eight; to San Jose, where it was fifty-three; and to Virginia Beach, where it was fifty-four. Source: American Community Survey, 2000, https://www.census.gov/programs-surveys/acs. I thank my colleagues Yung Chun and Stephen Roll from Washington University in St. Louis for compiling this data.

(one of the two was a single mother, who was supportive but could not finance it).

White respondents were more likely to have parents in manual labor or blue-collar occupations, such as truck-driving, while African American parents were more likely to be caretakers, medical assistants, operators and/or logistical assistants, or unemployed (with the fathers more likely to be unemployed and/or missing than the mothers). There was also evidence of some grandparents serving in caretaker roles for African Americans but not for whites.

What is also striking are the differences on the white and Black responses on the Cantril ladder—both present and future. As in the case of our larger N data from the Gallup surveys of adults, Black respondents were much more likely to score higher on the future ladder than white ones (and tended to score higher on the ladder today), suggesting different levels of hope for the future. These may reflect some cultural response bias, but as we have explored in the larger N surveys, the same optimistic Black respondents are still realistic and are much more critical of their financial situations and the places they live than whites.

Our Black respondents were more likely to volunteer, to do community service, to trust their neighbors, and have friends and family they could rely on in times of need. At the same time, they were also more likely than whites to carry a weapon to stay safe in their neighborhoods. Crime seemed to be a concern for all respondents. Only a few respondents reported to have been beaten up or hurt, which was surprisingly likely to be from within their families and was more likely among white respondents.

Risky or unsafe sex does not seem to be a major problem—or at least the respondents do not report it to be, and only one respondent reported to have had sex when she did not want to. Several respondents were not yet sexually active, but for the most part seemed educated about birth control and unsafe sex.

On the one hand, our findings are hopeful, as the low-income African American respondents see education as a way to improve their lives, believing it will pay off in the end. On the other hand, the low education aspirations of the white respondents—and the lack of parental support for achieving education beyond high school—is likely to result in another generation of low-income whites in despair, as a high school education alone is insufficient for the next generation to navigate tomorrow's labor markets (or even today's).

What also stands out in the differences across the racial groups is the key role of mentorship/parental support. It is difficult to remain hopeful about the future in adverse circumstances in the absence of some support and knowledge of the available opportunities. What is clear in the surveys is that adolescents lack information on available opportunities and on what skills they need to take advantage of those opportunities. While parents may also have limited information, not supporting the hopes and aspirations of their children to get ahead seems surprising. (Chapter 5 reviews what we know about interventions designed to support hope and the important role of mentorship.)

Stories of Resilience and Dashed Hopes

While consistent general patterns have emerged across the respondents, some differences, regardless of the respondents' race or gender, are worth noting. For the most part, though, even when troubled, the respondents fit the same hopeful vs. nonhopeful patterns. The stories in this section are of hopes crushed by COVID-19 uncertainties; shocks due to illness; the costs of broken families; and some examples of remarkable resilience in the face of these. The names of the respondents have been changed to protect their anonymity.

Taylor is a twenty-year-old while male who moved to St. Louis from Tampa, Florida, about five years before we conducted the survey. He is disabled and not working, he has disability insurance and health insurance, and he worries a lot. He wants to move but has neither the skills nor finances to do so (a common theme for most respondents, regardless of race or gender). His mother wants him to attend college (rare among the white parents), but he thinks it is unlikely he will succeed. Taylor, his parents, and his friends all smoke. He has no real hope or ambitions for the future and seems lonely. He spends much of his time playing video games and he has just a few friends.

A similar story is told by Darius—a white male of Slavic origin. He is in good health, unlike Taylor, and that reflects in his higher ladder scores (seven today, nine in the past, and eight in the future). His mother wants him to attend college, but he is not very hopeful. While he gets along somewhat with his parents, he does not make friends easily. He is aware of what unsafe sex is and he does not smoke, but he drinks and occasionally smokes marijuana. He has a strong locus of control and seems to be in control of his limited future. Like Taylor's, his is a rather lonely and limited vision, without a sense of a future.

Another white male, Devin, aged eighteen, has lived in St. Louis his entire life. His mother and father have high school and college degrees, respectively. He is a high school student and would like to work but cannot find a job. He is lonely, reports some depression, is unhappy, and does not have many friends. He does not get along with his parents and has been beaten up by a family member. He worries a lot but does not smoke, drink, or take drugs, and he is not sexually active (he is also quite uneducated about sexual matters). He does think about the future and what his career might be, and he has a strong internal locus of control. Like many of the white respondents, his vision for the future is more individually oriented than community-oriented, and he does not want to seek out support from family or friends.

The more hopeful and community-backed visions of most of the African American respondents contrast with the narratives above. Ashley, for example, is a nineteen-year-old woman who loves her family and is very hopeful about the future. Her ladder scores are eight today, ten in the past, and ten in the future. She says her mother, a telephone operator with a high school education, has supported her in her schooling and wants her to attend college, although both COVID-19 uncertainties and finances are concerns. Her father is unemployed. She gets along with both parents and enjoys being with family and doing sports. She smokes, does not drink, but enjoys marijuana.

Similarly, Jamiya, aged eighteen, is very hopeful. Her ladder scores are eight today, five in the past, and ten in the future. She plans to get an associate degree and thinks she can achieve it. She does not worry much and spends a considerable amount of time volunteering and doing community service. She is sexually active but also educated and uses birth control. She gets along well with her parents, friends, and family.

Antoine, a nineteen-year-old male, fits the same trend. His ladder scores are ten, ten, and ten! He is a high school student and in a work-training program and plans to get a technical degree. Both his parents have less than a high school degree but support his efforts. He volunteers a lot and gets along with his parents. He also would like to move—in large part due to crime—but his family is here. He has no money but saves what he can and thinks about the future. He gets happiness from family, friends, and sports.

Devon, meanwhile, is also a nineteen-year-old male. He is hopeful about the future although the present is full of unpleasant work and uncertainty. He is a high school graduate and works twenty to forty hours per week, with an uncertain schedule, and earns about fifteen thousand to twenty thousand dollars per year. He has a social security card but does not have health insurance. He hopes to obtain a college degree, and his grandparent—who was most involved in his schooling—is a supporter. He has friends, loves sports, and gets along reasonably well with his parents (neither of whom finished high school). He has a strong locus of control and believes in his future. He is sexually savvy, educated, and generally does not worry much.

Another example is Dariya, a nineteen-year-old woman who is in strong control of her future, despite having had negative shocks. Her ladder scores are eight today, six in the past, and nine in the future. Her mother has some college education and works as a nurse. Her father had less than a high school education and is deceased, sometime after divorcing and abandoning his family. Dariya is not bothered by much; she finished high school and works full-time; she aspires to attain a college degree and go to graduate school, and her mother supports her in these goals. Finances and COVID-19 uncertainties are concerns, as they are for most respondents of the survey. She works over forty hours a week, does domestic chores, and spends a lot of time with friends and in sports. She does not want to move, as her family is here. She makes friends easily, has the support of her family and gets along with them, and is very hopeful about the future. Dariya is sexually aware and educated but is not active yet. Family—and shopping—keep her happy.

Gabriela is a twenty-year-old Hispanic woman with college-educated parents—her mother is a teacher and her father is a CPA. Both parents want her to attend college. She was, until recently, a full-time student and financed by her parents' savings and by loans. She has been injured and ill but remains hopeful and reports her health as basically good. She saves what she can, she has a strong locus of control, and she is confident she can complete her bachelor's degree. Her family and friends make her happy.

There are also some examples of despair/loneliness among African American respondents, but they are indeed the exception. Even then, they still seem to retain some hope for a better future. One African American woman, aged nineteen, developed a phobia during COVID-19 and blames the virus for her not wanting to socialize with anyone. Her ladder scores are far lower than most African American respondents, with a three at present, a two in the past, and a six in the future (at least indicating she hopes things will improve). She lives alone with her mother, who supports her getting a college degree. And while she doubts her future prospects, she does talk with both her parents and believes she can solve her problems.

Why Such Different Visions of the Future?

Is it at all possible to generalize? I am relying on intuition based on a small but consistent set of life stories and personal testimonies, though I am used to finding statistical regularities in large data sets. It seems risky. Yet the patterns are consistent—both within this sample and with other larger studies, including our own, that have documented these differences. What stands out is hope in the face of obstacles among most of the minority respondents, particularly African Americans, and stubborn individualism mixed with lack of real ability to change things or get ahead among low-income young whites.

The patterns are also supported by different kinds of evidence, such as in the historical pattern of African American optimism and resilience in the face of slavery, followed by persistent discrimination, to renewed discussions about structural racism, in part triggered by the Black Lives Matter movement. The latter seems to have negative effects on wealthier and more educated young African Americans than it does among low-income ones, perhaps because they are more aware of—and more likely to reach—the glass ceilings that still exist. The starkest reminder of this is the 2019 and 2020 increase in minority teen suicides—which are much more likely among the highly educated than noneducated. There is also recent work by Tiffany Ford on the paradox of middle-class Black women's positive reported well-being compared to their poor objective health metrics (and, in particular, high levels of diabetes and heart disease), while wealthier Black women are both healthier and wealthier but have lower optimism scores.[2]

Is this adaptation and coping, or is it something else? Our earlier research suggests it is more complicated than just adapting to adversity, although that is likely at play. When we explored the scores of the same surprisingly optimistic low-income respondents, we found they were very realistic and much more negative when asked to evaluate their financial situations and their satisfaction with the places they live (although they are more likely to want to improve their communities than other racial cohorts).[3] Hope and resilience seem to coexist with unpleasant realities and with frustration with a system that continues to discriminate. Indeed, in mid-2020, at the height of the COVID-19 pandemic and the protests surrounding the murder of George Floyd, while anxiety increased among African Americans, it coexisted with the highest levels of optimism of any racial cohort.[4]

There are also stronger cultural norms that stigmatize suicide—considered weakness or giving up—among both African Americans and Hispanics than among whites, which affect both suicide rates and reporting of these deaths. Analogous to this, there is often surprise at the data that shows that the Scandinavian countries have high rates of suicide

2 Assari et al. (2018); Ford (2022).
3 Graham (2017); Blanchflower and Oswald (2019); and Graham and Pinto (2021).
4 Graham, Chun, et al. (2022).

compared to other European countries like Spain, France, or Italy. Yet the numbers do not take into account the differences in cultural norms, which again affect both the rate and the reporting of these deaths.

That, in turn, is further complicated by trends during the pandemic. The year 2020 showed an initial increase and then a decline in suicides compared to 2019 in the United States, yet this was accompanied by a major increase of drug overdose deaths among all groups—and at unprecedented rates, albeit starting at much lower levels, among minority men. It is notoriously difficult to disentangle intentional from nonintentional overdose deaths, with estimates for intentional overdose deaths ranging from 15–60% of total overdose deaths.[5]

These trends coexist with rising levels of despair among less-than-college-educated whites in the past two decades. While the deaths of despair were first reported by Anne Case and Angus Deaton in their seminal 2015 article, and then further documented in their 2017 article and their 2020 book, white despair began well before it showed up in the death rates, along with the decline of manufacturing firms, the white working class, and the communities that supported it beginning in the 1970s.

Kelsey O'Connor and I found that African American and female optimism levels rose in the late 1970s, along with improved gender and civil rights. At the same time, also marked by the first declines in manufacturing, less-than-high-school-educated white men (whose education demographic was equivalent to less-than-college-educated men today) began to drop in their optimism levels.[6]

White despair—and the decline of the white working class—has been the subject of many recent books, including

---

5 We discuss this in detail in Dobson et al., forthcoming.
6 O'Connor and Graham (2019).

Arlie Hosthchild's *Strangers in Their Own Land*, J.D. Vance's *Hillbilly Elegy*, and Jennifer Silva's *We're Still Here: Pain and Politics in the Heart of America*. In the same communities where jobs and opportunities faded, as did the families and other associations that supported and depended on them, an entire way of life disappeared.

In the last twenty years, marriage rates among low-income whites have fallen more than any other cohort and now are the same as low-income minorities. Marriage rates in the United States are now, like many other things, distributed unequally, with the wealthy and college-educated, regardless of race, much more likely to be married than the poor and less educated. Indeed, while marriage rates have increased slightly among wealthy, dual-earning couples, there has been an increase in single-headed households among low-income groups, which is part of the explanation for our remarkable increases in inequality over the past two decades.[7]

In addition to this was the perfect storm of the opioid epidemic—which affected whites the worst, in part because they were more likely to report pain and to be prescribed opioids than minorities. Opioid use—and reported pain—in the United States increased dramatically from the year 2000 on,[8] partly because of supply and partly because of the resulting demand. It is difficult to tell what was behind the increases in reported pain among less-than-college-educated, middle-aged whites. Was it a reaction to actual pain increases or to psychological pain as their life narrative was challenged? Was it driven by opioids? Or a combination of all these factors? Ironically, the actual discrimination that minorities experienced in pain treatment ended up being protective during the opioid epidemic.

---

7 Burtless (2009).
8 Quinones (2015); Blanchflower and Oswald (2019); Graham and Pinto (2019); and Case, Deaton, and Stone (2021).

Over these same decades, there was also a widening geographic rift in the country, which has since become a cultural rift. While the country's coasts grew more diverse, economically vibrant, and denser in population, the heartland experienced a decline in population, economic activity, quality and quantity of education, and civic activity. In much of the heartland, the decline in median wages and employment rates has been staggering. Even health is now largely determined by location, with huge disparities in life expectancy and other indicators, which used to be starker across races than place.[9]

The exception is a handful of relatively well-endowed small cities, so-called comeback towns. They capitalized on the investments of large firms looking for hubs and production sites outside the large and expensive coastal cities where they are headquartered. If the cities have basic education and transportation infrastructure, such as community colleges and a nearby airport, they have experienced recent economic revivals.[10] While these comeback towns surely provide some grounds for hope, there are also some communities that have no realistic chance of coming back, and the next generation has to move away to find a stable economic existence.

Andrew Cherlin, a sociologist at Johns Hopkins, conducted an ethnographic study of the children of the steelworkers at the Bethlehem Steel mills in Baltimore. He shows how these stories have played out across races and highlights the different hopes and beliefs in higher education, among other things. Cherlin tells the story of segregation and discrimination at the mills in detail, with the African American steel workers being brought in from North Carolina, living in segregated housing, and relegated to inferior jobs and

9 Robert Wood Johnson Foundation (2014).
10 Atkinson, Muro, and Whiton (2019).

lower rates of promotion even though civil rights laws were newly established.[11]

Regardless, the Black steel workers for the most part stayed in their jobs and saved for their children's education to provide them with better futures. Most of their children attended college and moved away from Dundalk, the large town adjacent to Baltimore harbor where the steel workers lived and raised their families, and ended up in more prosperous parts of northern Baltimore, such as Towson. An equally important part of the story, which resonates with the tales told in the rest of the chapter, is that after moving away they regularly returned to their childhood neighborhood to attend church and give back to the community—the same community where the HBO television series of drugs and gangs in Baltimore—*The Wire*—was filmed.

In contrast, the children of the white steel workers did not tend to attend university and had downward mobility compared to their parents. Most still live in Dundalk and work in jobs in the gig economy or driving taxis in the area, upset at the arrival of Section 8 housing and immigrants in Dundalk. While they are not necessarily politically radicalized, they do not see a better path for themselves or their children. Neurologists have identified one's lack of hope for the future—a component of despair—as a key vulnerability in the face of false information, conspiracy theories, and radicalization.[12]

New York Times reporter Thomas Edsall, in a series of stories on the disgruntlement, decline, and political radicalization of the white working class, writes how the downward mobility of this cohort has been used to justify conspiracy theories, racialized politics, and the January 6 riots on the Capitol.[13]

11 Cherlin (2019).

12 See the discussion on despair and radicalization in the Brookings report on despair and economic recovery in chapter 2.

13 Edsall (2021a, 2021b).

Indeed, President Donald Trump capitalized on this disaffection and lack of vision for the future, using it to build his base and ultimately erode faith in democracy. While some former Trump supporters have detected his bluff and realized that, in the end, he did nothing to help them, an equally large if not larger number of them voted to reelect Trump in 2020 and continue to believe that the 2020 election was stolen.

While the political division and threat to our governance is frightening and real, it has been well documented elsewhere and is beyond my expertise. Yet it is related to the differential hopes and beliefs in the future I find in my research. We must solve our national political and civic impasse to restore faith in and appreciation of our long-held democratic form of governance. It is hard to imagine restoring hope among disaffected youths if we cannot reestablish some form of confidence in the future of our society and how it is governed, laws are made, and truth is established.[14]

Conclusion

These rifts are very much a part of the challenges facing the young today. It is hard enough to navigate changing labor markets, but on top of that, youths must navigate a pandemic that has had disastrous effects on those markets, and especially on the kinds of jobs available to the young and unskilled, all the while facing the difficulties of financing decent education and health care. When coupled with a lack of trust in the political system, education, science, civic society, and even in one's neighbors, what you get is what we have—a divided, mistrusting, and broken society—which makes it even more difficult for the young to chart a course forward.

14 For an informative and thoughtful review, see Jonathan Rauch's recently published book on what constitutes truth and how consensus on that has faded (2021).

How can the next generation navigate this? How can we use whatever skills and knowledge we have to help them do so? How do we deal with such different beliefs across citizens of the same country? We are, indeed, at a critical moment. The different visions of the future that our surveys give us are stark. Once you also consider what is actually happening in everyday lives—antivaccine campaigns, lawsuits over mask mandates, adults attacking other adults because their personal space is violated on commercial airplane fights—it is hard to craft a shared vision. In addition, we have our crisis of gun violence, which the pandemic exacerbated, and different beliefs on what constitutes police brutality, fair elections, and basic civil liberties.[15] Given all this, it is difficult to make any sense or have any confidence in where we are going as a society. What are those just entering our society as young adults supposed to think, much less do?

While there is a debate over how much the pandemic has harmed mental health over the past two years, there are credible signs that the young are suffering from mental health problems more than they have before, and that the stark signs of despair we have seen in our society for decades are now surfacing among young adults.[16]

At the least, we can do our best to encourage young adults—particularly those facing more uncertain and less privileged futures—to invest in the kinds of education and skills that are likely to provide them with opportunities and better fu-

15 Our recent analysis of EMS data, comparing trends in social ills in 2020 to 2019, finds a significant increase in gun violence. The results of other studies support our analysis.

16 In recent research, we found that estimates of how much depression and anxiety had increased among the eighteen to twenty-five age cohort varied a great deal, depending on the survey and the survey instruments used to assess the trends. While that does not mean an absence of troubling signs and trends in our nation's mental health, it does make us cautious in putting exact numbers on the problem. See Dobson et al. (2022) for a discussion and a comparison across findings with different questions and different surveys.

tures than they are now envisioning. It is hard to imagine a coherent society with such different visions of what the future brings.

While detailed interventions and policies are the subject of the next chapter, some tangible lessons emerge from the surveys in Peru and Missouri. One is that hope is not only possible in deprived populations but is essential to their overcoming their situations. Lack of hope, in contrast, is a vicious circle, with desperation overwhelming the traits and attributes that underlie hope and are linked to its agentic properties. Those who have hope, as seen in the surveys, tend to believe they can overcome their problems—and seek support and help in doing so—while those who do not are more doubtful about the future, less trusting of others, and therefore less likely to seek help.

That raises a more difficult question: How do we restore hope among populations where it has been lost? A major challenge is drawing lessons across populations that have different attitudes about the role of individuals versus communities, and the kind of support and knowledge the latter can provide. Mentorship is key, but how does one establish viable mentors—and acceptance of them—in places and populations where there is little experience with and trust in them?

In the next chapter, I review some experiences and experiments that aim to increase hope and related aspirations among cohorts who lack them. Some of this is in the mental health sphere—it is difficult to increase aspirations among those who are in despair, and solving that challenge is, indeed, an essential first step. Yet, as little as we know about hope, restoring it—including the ability to value and help oneself—is also a part of the solution. Reducing isolation and despair is important, but so is creating a path to a better future, particularly for the young, who have most of their lives ahead of them.

Lessons from the nascent well-being literature show the benefits of pulling isolated, desperate people into their communities and into community activities and, at the same time, teaching young people coping skills and how to train and prepare for existing opportunities. Perhaps this is an area where psychiatrists and psychologists on the one hand, and economists and behavioral scientists on the other, can learn from one another for the greater good. And we still have a lot to learn.

There is a lot we do not know, but we can draw lessons from recent experience. And as social science techniques become more sophisticated and incorporate human behavior, genetic endowments, and the intersection between the brain and the environment, we have tools we could not have dreamed of even fifty years ago. If one of the most prosperous nations in the world—and one of its longest lasting democracies—cannot restore hope in the dreams that made it thrive in the first place, then we are looking at a grim future for our country and for liberal democracy in general.

CHAPTER 5

Can Hope Be Restored in Populations and Places Where It Has Been Lost?

Despair is a state where one does not care whether one lives or dies, where the will for change for the better has been lost, and where the narrative of one's life is gone, with nothing to replace it. It is the analogue of hope, which combines the sense that things can get better with the will to make them better. How do people get from one state to the other? Why has this happened on a large scale in one of the wealthiest countries on earth? What can be done?

In the United States, as is grimly demonstrated by at least a million despair-related deaths since 2005, entire communities have lost their raison d'etre, their social fabric, and any sense of a better future. Almost 100,000 people died of overdose deaths alone in 2020, when the COVID-19 pandemic exacerbated the preexisting crisis of despair. These same communities tend to have a high concentration of prime-aged males out of the labor force, especially white working-class men. It has resulted in geographic clusters where significant parts of the population do not have the aspirations, skills, or health to move to jobs elsewhere, even if they are available in relatively nearby places. Deaths of despair tend to follow.

Lack of investment and pervasive hopelessness are a vicious circle in which individuals *and* their communities enter a spiral of decline. Addressing this issue requires connecting the mental health treatment side of the problem with community revival and resilience efforts. For the most part, these operate as separate worlds. It also requires acknowledging the difficulties inherent in identifying how white men are suffering while at the same time recognizing they are in many ways privileged.

It is worth noting that some of the problems faced by the declining U.S. white working class are likely faced by many working-class populations in other countries—including poor ones—as the nature of economies and jobs changes dramatically due to technology-driven growth. There is no longer a stable work-life narrative for those who do not acquire higher education or technical skills. In the United States, this is compounded by a drug overdose crisis, widely available guns, racial tensions, starkly unequal access to health care (the allocation of which is often determined by resources rather than need), and a civil society divided by income, education gaps, and political beliefs, including a rise in right-wing radicalization.

The problem is complex and there are no magic bullets. Yet important lessons have emerged from a range of disciplines (economics, psychology, psychiatry, and public health) that can help address it. Instead of thinking of these lessons in terms of disciplines, it is perhaps more useful to think of them from the perspective of shared objectives. Most successful policies and interventions that aim to restore hope have similar objectives, which can serve as general guideposts for such efforts.

A basic first step is to reduce the kinds of uncertainties that make the future, as well as planning for it and investing in it, out of reach and essentially impossible. They are common to people who live in extreme poverty, as living hand-to-mouth and day-to-day makes it difficult to plan. The poor in the United States, who often have limited access to health care and stable jobs, face similar uncertainties (surprising in one of the world's wealthiest countries). As eloquently described by Sendhil Mullainathan and Eldar Shafir (2013) in their book *Scarcity*, this uncertainty has long-term cognitive effects on people's ability to think and plan, which affects everything from acquiring education to preserving one's health to saving for the future.

Recent research along these lines demonstrates the efficacy of cash transfers (targeted ones) in improving health equity outcomes—from reductions in hospitalization rates, psychological distress, incidences of psychiatric disorders, and depression.[1] Given the rise of the gig economy, unemployment risks posed by automation, and the fluctuating nature of wage labor, a 2017 report by the Pew Charitable Trust estimates that income volatility—an annual income fluctuation of 25% or more, which already impacts nearly half the U.S. population—is likely to continue influencing health outcomes, highlighting the inextricable link between public health and economic stability.

Being unable to plan makes it difficult to have agency over the future. It is particularly difficult for the young if they have no hope and no one to support their aspirations. This was evident in the surveys we fielded among low-income adolescents in Missouri. There was a big difference in the future-oriented behaviors of those with hopes and aspirations—and with a mentor to support them—than those without, regardless of material circumstances. Indeed, rather ironically, it was minority adolescents, who are usually more materially deprived, who were more hopeful and more likely to invest in their future education than the children of those in the white working class.

Most of these adolescents did not know what tomorrow's labor markets—and the skills needed to navigate them—look like. This is a more common challenge for poor youths, who

1 Forget (2011); Baird, de Hoop, and Özler (2013); Dieter et al. (2013); Powell-Jackson et al. (2016); and Aizer, Eli, Ferrie, and Lleras-Muney (2016).

are often knowledge-poor as well as income-poor in comparison to their wealthier peers.

Restoring hope (or overcoming despair) requires reducing uncertainty, but it also must restore individuals' self-confidence, agency, and trust in others. While this is obviously a process that requires individual change, it benefits from community involvement. People who are already in despair are unlikely to seek out help. Often, people in their community are more effective at reaching out to them or at least identifying risk than professionals who are unlikely to be familiar with their community.

Recognizing the trauma that has occurred at the collective level is a beginning. So is engaging the people of a community in recasting their narratives, this time with a focus on their strengths and capacities. Creating programs that promote resiliency are a natural outgrowth of this. This can be as simple as getting isolated and/or depressed individuals who are unlikely to reenter the labor market out of isolation via programs that encourage volunteering and participating in the arts and group activities outdoors. Addressing loneliness and isolation is a critical first step.

Reaching the next generation, though, requires supporting them in developing the tools they need to participate in new labor markets. This requires access to new skills-acquisition and to information about available opportunities. These opportunities do not always require a college education, but rather an understanding of the skills needed to participate in new kinds of jobs (such as medium technology programming or soft skills that are increasingly important in the changing service sector).

Yet without hope *and* agency—which often requires the support of a mentor—it is unlikely that young adults in deprived communities will take up opportunities, even when they exist. My survey research suggests that having either a parent or a community member who supports the educational aspirations of young adults is key to their achieving them, while not having this support is a substantial barrier to success.[2] Among low-income cohorts, minority parents are more supportive of their children pursuing higher education than white ones. (In addition to finding these patterns in my surveys, these patterns are also confirmed on a much larger scale, according to detailed conversations with the heads of Historically Black Colleges and Universities in late 2019.)

While the problem seems daunting, there are a variety of ways in which individuals from all walks of life can provide the critical mentorship that helps young adults in deprived or fading communities avoid their parents' fates. These include setting up networks that link high schools in deprived areas with schools in other parts of the country, via virtual joint classes; creating new contacts for students; and sharing best practices among teachers. These networks can also link schools with local colleges and businesses to expose students to college-level courses and job-placement schemes, along with providing students advice on next steps on the educational and career ladder. Equally important is encouraging private-sector professionals and their companies to establish long-term volunteering and sponsorship relationships with schools and community organizations in struggling regions, where connections and relevant information are scarce.[3]

Increasingly, in part due to the challenges posed by COVID-19, the mental health community is creating "communities of care" as a first step to getting people with mental health problems to seek support. Significant regions of states, particularly rural ones, do not have access to mental health care. Yet there are ways, including telehealth, to provide new forms

2 Graham and Ruiz-Pozuelo (2021).
3 Hill (2021).

of health care, and community members can play a big role in getting those in despair to seek them out.[4]

For example, conditions that we consider simple problems —such as loneliness—are emotional states that are often linked to serious mental health illnesses such as depression. Combating loneliness is much more effective than turning depression around once it has set in, and it does not require medical care. A recent study in the U.K. by Andrew Steptoe and colleagues estimates that one in five depression cases could be solved by strategies to combat loneliness. And government policies can support such efforts at a low cost, as the approach of the U.K. government and the resulting "minister of loneliness" demonstrate (discussed in detail below).

More generally, COVID-19, although tragic, has created awareness among governments to take these problems seriously by prioritizing societal well-being and economic prosperity. The impact of COVID-19 was similar across many rich countries, with increases in reported depression and anxiety, although the characteristics of vulnerable groups differ. Mental health and loneliness are worse among the most vulnerable, with young adults and people with low incomes disproportionately at risk. Those who are vulnerable—due to losing a job, having difficulty accessing food, or an inability to pay bills— have the worst *objective experiences* and also suffer additional negative effects on mental health due to high levels of worry.[5] Poor mental health was also negatively related to compliance with government guidelines during the pandemic.

The death toll in poor countries is typically even higher than in rich countries, given extensive poverty and greater difficulty associated with social distancing. Gallup World Poll data finds that 2020 was the year with the most reported

4 See, for example, Unützer et al. (2013). See also: www.chcs.org/media/HH _IRC_Collaborative_Care_Model__052113_2.pdf and http://wellbeingtrust.org/.
5 Graham (2020).

stress since the poll became active in 2005, with reported stress increasing from 35% to 40% among poll respondents. The highest levels of stress were reported in poor countries with high COVID-19 instances, with hard-hit Peru at the top of the list, with 66% of respondents reporting experiencing stress the previous day (Mastrangelo 2021). Thus, the policies discussed below can apply to a range of country contexts.

Well-being metrics are tools for the moment. Measuring well-being gives us a lens into the emotional and mental health costs associated with the pandemic and some strategies to ameliorate those costs. Well-being metrics allow us to assess how trends in life satisfaction, hope, anxiety, and depression compare for the same population groups before and after COVID-19. Well-being data reflects actual trends and can be predictive of future behaviors. We find that ill-being markers— such as despair and stress—are strongly associated with the probability of dying from deaths of despair (both for individuals and places). The increase in despair preceded the increase in deaths by two decades, suggesting a possible predictive role. We are now using the metrics as warning indicators of overdoses, suicides, and other despair-related deaths.[6]

Societies cannot completely recover from the pandemic if their populations are in poor and deteriorating mental health. We regularly take stock of the state of our economies via rates of interest, inflation, and unemployment. Why can't we also regularly take society's temperature, so to speak, to gauge its well-being? The dire nature of the situation in many countries makes this task even more important. And, as noted above, it is increasingly recognized that higher levels of well-being and productivity go hand in hand.[7]

6 See Graham and Pinto (2019); O'Connor and Graham (2019); and our recently updated vulnerability indicator, "Geography of Hope and Desperation in America": https://www.brookings.edu/interactives/wellbeing-interactive/.

7 See De Neve and Oswald (2012); Proto and Oswald (2016); Graham et al. (2004); and Nikolova and Cnossen (2021).

There is a wide body of academic research on the causes and consequences of well-being.[8] Health (especially mental health), having a spouse or partner, and social relationships account for more than three-quarters of the explained variance in adult people's life satisfaction.[9] Evidence also suggests that well-being is a significant predictor of important life and economic outcomes, including health and longevity, productivity and income, voting, and even compliance with lockdown measures during COVID-19.[10]

We have more experience with targeted interventions and policies to raise the well-being of those who are suffering (a necessary objective, as I emphasize throughout this book), but we have less experience with policies or programs that improve the well-being of the entire population in general. Challenges include ensuring that governments are not in the business of telling people how to be happy; there are also issues of generalizability and scalability across large populations.[11] A few countries, though, such as the U.K. and New Zealand, have placed general well-being at the center of their policy priorities, including in the budget arena. Their experience is likely to receive more attention since countries around the world have faced COVID-19 and the challenges it has posed to societies' health and mental well-being.

An important related effort is investing in the next generation and in the future of jobs. We should not just put out fires of despair (although at present we clearly must). We also need to prepare the next generation to lead healthier, more

8 See, among many others, Blanchflower and Oswald (2004); Clark et al. (2018); Diener et al. (1999); Frey and Stutzer (2002); Graham (2009); and Layard (2005).

9 Clark et al. (2018); Krekel et al. (2021).

10 On longevity, see Steptoe and Wardle (2001); Graham and Pinto (2019). On productivity and income, see De Neve and Oswald (2012); Graham et al. (2004); and Oswald et al. (2015). On voting, see Liberini et al. (2017); Pinto et al. (2020). On COVID-19 compliance, see Krekel et al. (2020).

11 See Graham and MacLennan (2020) for a discussion of these.

productive, happier lives, and that requires investing in the skills they will need to navigate future labor markets. As low-skill jobs dwindle and deteriorate in quality, we need to teach different skills. Cognitive skills—which include personality traits—will become more and more important. And these skills can be learned and enhanced far later in the life course than abstract reasoning power, which determines IQ, as research by James Heckman and Tim Kautz finds (discussed in detail in chapter 3).

While reducing the isolation and despair of the current working (or better put, not working) prime-age population is a necessity to avoid more calamities today, it is perhaps even more important to address the uncertainties and educational needs of the next generation. If the youths of today do not train and invest in critical skills now, they will end up as the next generation in despair. They need guidance, mentors, and community support to acquire those skills, as our survey research and the work of some others makes abundantly clear.

The examples described in the remainder of the chapter range from interventions in well-being, mental health support, creativity and the arts, community-level efforts, and private-public partnerships. Addressing these issues has the important objective of enhancing societal well-being and mental health at a time of an unprecedented global pandemic and also of helping to prevent a radicalization of politics and a rejection of democratic norms in many countries. Most of these interventions, meanwhile, are not country-specific, but, when successful, can be transported across borders and per capita income levels.

Well-Being Interventions

A range of simple interventions are effective at increasing the well-being of individuals and communities (which are distinct from country-level policies). While there are too many programs to detail them all here, the following are examples of programs that can make a small-cost and high-benefit difference at a generalizable and scalable level. More detail on programs and interventions is available on the website of the What Works Centre for Wellbeing in the U.K., which was established as part of the government's efforts to include well-being as a policy priority. As such, the U.K. treasury includes well-being metrics in its evaluations and cost-benefits analyses of policy operations.

The What Works Centre, now directed by Nancy Hey, sponsors the design, implementation, and evaluation (for cost-benefit and scalability purposes) of interventions designed to enhance individual and community-level well-being.[12] Things as simple as providing opportunities for volunteering, access to the arts, or even group walks in green spaces can enhance well-being by reducing loneliness and depressive symptoms among isolated community members, often those who are either out of work, elderly, or both. Simply getting people out of isolation and into some sort of purposeful activity is a positive step to reducing despair. Equally important, the center's work and findings are available as public goods and are part of the discussions on how best to incorporate well-being into policy decisions in government agencies.[13]

There are also some important lessons from bottom-up, place-based solutions, many of which emphasize the assets

12 For full disclosure, I have served on their advisory board for almost a decade.

13 See the homepage of What Works Wellbeing. The center has been involved in a promising new program, the Greater Manchester Young People's Wellbeing Project, which assesses well-being and its drivers for eighth and tenth grade students across the city, forty thousand young people for three years. A critical part of project is assessing "life readiness," and includes as key variables optimism, hope for a better life, and similar metrics. See https://uomseed.com /beewell-neighbourhoods/2021/.

that communities have and can build on. The City of Santa Monica introduced the first municipal project to define, measure, and improve community well-being, led by Julie Rusk and supported by a Bloomberg Philanthropies grant. That effort used an annual citywide well-being survey and index to reframe a host of municipal priorities and policies, including budgetary policy. The effort addressed deep inequities in health, income, and well-being across race and income groups in Santa Monica. Involving the community in decisions about its own solutions was an important part of the process. As noted in several examples below, having hope and a sense of belonging and trust in the community help explain the success of small enterprises and artists in these difficult times.[14]

Another more recent, large-scale initiative is the U.K. Levelling Up program, which has a wide array of policies to address the diverse needs of deprived communities. Its umbrella objective is enhancing well-being in the country more generally, while its explicit focus is to increase the average levels of life satisfaction in the country and to reduce their dispersion across communities and places.

Some new efforts aim to enhance well-being at the community level rather than focus on vulnerable groups. Christian Krekel and colleagues (2021) conducted a randomized controlled trial of a scalable social-psychological intervention rooted in self-determination theory and aimed at raising the well-being and prosociality of the general adult population. The program, Exploring What Matters, is run by lay volunteers in their local communities and, to date, has been conducted in more than twenty-six countries. The authors found that it had strong, positive causal effects on participants' subjective well-being and prosociality (compassion

14 See https://www.santamonicawellbeing.org.

and social trust) while improving indicators of poor mental health.[15]

Exploring What Matters also differs from most existing interventions in two critical aspects: first, the course is led by nonexpert volunteers rather than trained clinicians; second, because of the program's cost-savings and its more general objective, it is more scalable than many interventions. The course brings together participants in focus groups to discuss what matters for a happy, meaningful, and virtuous life. Participants span a wide range of ages and socioeconomic backgrounds but can be broadly classified, as per their self-reports, into two categories: people who are unhappy and looking for ways to improve their lives; and people who are interested in well-being more generally and want to learn more. The sessions build on a theme—such as, what matters in life or how to find meaning at work—which is then discussed through a frame and background of scientific evidence on the topics (distinct from telling people how to be happy).

Psychological self-determination theory (Deci and Ryan 1985) posits that autonomy, relatedness, and competence are fundamental human needs that enable people to achieve well-being. The Exploring What Matters course aims to build the following: first, autonomy, by enabling participants to discover what matters in their lives, accompanied by a section that introduces scientific evidence on that week's theme; second, relatedness, by facilitating interpersonal connections and social trust within the gathering; and third, competence, via participants experiencing how changes in daily routines can make differences to their and others' well-being.

---

15 One additional challenge to this approach (which much of the evidence in the literature *does not* support) is that increasing well-being in general is unlikely to last, at least if individuals have a "set point" or fixed level of well-being around which changes fluctuate. There is still debate over the existence of a set point, with the balance of the evidence in contrary. See Brickman and Campbell (1971).

Program evaluations (based on the U.K. interventions) yielded increases in average life satisfaction and social trust scores and decreases in reported anxiety and depression (based on the PH2–9 and GAD-7 screening questions) compared to the control group (potential participants who had applied but not yet gotten into the program).

An intervention that is quite different but also relies on involving communities in their own revival does so by involving parents of different backgrounds in their children's sport and art activities and then linking those activities to investments in their future education. Portland Community Squash, an initiative based on access to sports, the arts, and education, seeks to integrate immigrants and other deprived groups into the city via the provision of support for K-12 education, mentorship, and help navigating the college entrance process. The basis in sports and in the friendships and ties that the young participants make has helped parents from diverse backgrounds integrate into what used to be a homogenous white community. In the end, the aim is to increase hope, aspirations, well-being, and community coherence. The experiment is now being scaled up in several cities around the United States.[16]

Another new area of focus—in part spurred by challenges posed by COVID-19—is addressing loneliness as a priority. The What Works Centre for Wellbeing,[17] meanwhile, has a strong repository of knowledge on loneliness and has conducted its own studies.

A critical feature of loneliness is not having someone you can rely on in times of need, which is critical to well-being. Loneliness is different from solitude (a choice) and from social isolation (a condition, not an emotion). Loneliness is an emotion that is associated with despair, dementia, and low

16 https://www.pcsquash.com/.
17 https://whatworkswellbeing.org.

levels of well-being, among other facets of mental illness. While the pandemic has worsened loneliness, those who were already lonely displayed these traits well before. While loneliness does not necessarily cause depression, it is associated with it, in part because lonely people are likely to lose brain function more rapidly than the average person.

In 2021, the National Institute for Health Research launched a commission to study loneliness in older adults. The COVID-19 pandemic introduced the way that lonely older adults lived to a broader swath of the population. The study, led by Andrew Sharpe and colleagues and based on the U.K.'s English Longitudinal Study of Ageing, included many people who were lonely before the pandemic. The authors found that loneliness is not associated with age, social class, or social activities. Loneliness is, however, associated with prior loneliness, and the study estimates that dealing with loneliness could prevent one in five cases of depression in older adults.

There are also strong linkages between loneliness and low levels of well-being. Both share traits such as poor health, long-term illness or disability, unemployment, renting rather than owning a home, and being divorced or single. Being middle-aged is often the peak of low well-being, but youths are more likely to feel lonely. Low well-being is more prominent among men and those with low levels of education. In contrast, women tend to report more loneliness than men. Weak links to one's neighborhood or community and having little trust in others are associated with both loneliness and despair.

In part as a result of both Richard Layard's and Gus O'Donnell's successful efforts to get well-being and ill-being into government policy, the U.K. government has made loneliness a priority in its efforts in the well-being space. Prime Minister Theresa May followed up on the now deceased parliamentarian Jo Cox's efforts to combat loneliness by forming a commission to combat loneliness. In response to its recommendations, she appointed the government's first minister of loneliness, Tracey Crouch, and set up a crossgovernmental group responsible for crafting policies to address the growing problem.

Over nine million people of the U.K.'s population of sixty-six million report feeling lonely often or always, and over 200,000 elderly adults reported they had not had a conversation with a friend or relative in over a month. Meanwhile, the American Psychological Association reports that 40% of Americans over the age of forty-five suffer from chronic loneliness. In the United States thus far, government efforts have yet to follow. Government efforts in the U.K., though, have spawned several other efforts to address the problem, both in the public and the nonprofit sectors. As Theresa May noted at the time the loneliness program began, it was time for the government to help address the "sad reality of modern life" (Dasey 2018). Addressing loneliness before it manifests in depression and other more serious conditions is an example of how coordinated and timely well-being policy can prevent worse outcomes in the future. In the United States, we are seeing such outcomes in the forms of rising numbers of deaths of despair, at which point it is too late.

An equally important new initiative aims to teach soft and socioemotional skills in middle schools in the U.K. The Healthy Minds Initiative, which was piloted in a randomized control trial in thirty-four schools in relatively poor areas over four years, implemented a multiyear curriculum among middle and high school students that exposed them to curriculum specifically related to soft skills (as noted in chapter 2, soft skills have been shown to be malleable throughout the life course, well beyond the extent of cognitive skills).[18] The program evaluations showed it was effective in increasing emotional well-being, health, and behavior, with the strongest effects for boys (who tend to have weaker socioemotional

---

18 See Lordon and McGuire (2019); Heckman and Kautz (2013).

skills than girls). Some evidence suggests that the program increased occupational aspirations for the same cohorts. While new, the program has promise well beyond the U.K. and fits the broader objective of preparing youths for the labor markets of tomorrow, which are likely to emphasize such skills.

New Forms of Mental Health Support

Loneliness is at the intersection of well-being and mental health, which are related yet different concepts and conditions. People with low well-being are much more likely to suffer from mental health issues than those of average or above levels of well-being. Interventions to address low levels of well-being and interventions that have proven to be effective at improving mental health share certain traits. Before the pandemic, as deaths of despair highlighted the crisis of despair and other mental health illnesses in the United States, members of the mental health community, aware that the supply of care was well below the demand, experimented with novel forms of mental health support. Not surprisingly, on many levels, they resembled the traits of many successful well-being interventions.

In general, they aim to raise awareness and to provide support for accessing treatment, with communities of care playing an integral role. Telehealth is increasingly used to provide treatment, and new forms of community involvement are now playing a role in identifying risk (not diagnosing it). In the U.K., Richard Layard has long been an advocate of making cognitive behavioral therapy and other psychotherapies more widely available and has included that in his many efforts to advance well-being policy in the U.K. The Improving Access to Psychological Therapies program reaches approximately 500,000 patients per year and achieves recovery among 50% of them, while two-thirds see some sort of benefit. While cognitive behavioral therapy has its critics—particularly its use in the treatment of severe mental illness—making mental health care a priority for the government and more widely available was an important change in the U.K. and has led to more attention to the issue elsewhere.[19]

There are also efforts, particularly in the mental health arena, in the United States that could be taken to scale. Key to these efforts is integrating mental health and primary care. Primary care-based approaches can help detect and treat despair-driven mental health and substance use disorders earlier. The Collaborative Care Model (CoCM), for example, aims to improve overall health outcomes and has been proven to bend the cost curve, with the savings primarily derived by improvements in comorbid diseases that depression worsens, like diabetes and hypertension.[20] The Meadows Mental Health Policy Institute has modeled the potential effects of universal access to just two evidence-based treatments in primary care—CoCM for depression and medication-assisted treatment for addiction—and projects that this could save almost 40,000 lives a year from suicide (14,500) and overdose (24,000).[21]

Given that most mental health conditions emerge during school years, efforts to expand detection and early intervention in schools are promising. Efforts in Massachusetts and Texas that focused on urgent access have shown potential for rapid scaling.[22] Another proposal for universal depression screening in the Irvine school district in California is being pioneered by UC Irvine professor Rimal Bera.

---

19 For an assessment of its effectiveness and that of other expanded access psychotherapies, see Clark (2018). For a critique, see Marziller and Hall (2009).

20 Unützer et al. (2013).

21 Meadows Mental Health Policy Institute (2020).

22 Kessler et al. (2005). See https://mmhpi.org/wp-content/uploads/2019/10 /RoadmapAndToolkitForSchools.pdf; https://www.mamh.org/assets/files/V10 -URGENT-CARE-MODELS-Report.pdf; https://tcmhcc.utsystem.edu/tchatt/.

Well Being Trust, the Harvard School of Public Health, and several other organizations are collaborating to establish a new "theory of change" in this area by involving trusted community members—ranging from hairdressers to schoolteachers—to assess risk of mental health disorders in communities. The theory, in addition to cost-benefit and scalability, is that close community members are better positioned than trained technicians to see signs of change, distress, and other warning indicators. The first programs based on this theory are scheduled to launch in 2022.[23]

There are some examples of resilience centers, such as the resilience-based efforts within the Maryland Behavioral Health Administration's child and adolescent programs, which focus on lessons tailored to different age groups, from preschool through high school.[24] Integrated Community Therapy, a technology-based tool developed in Brazil, is a large-group approach to rebuilding and connecting people in a community around common life challenges. The approach is a promising basis for other public health interventions that go beyond the dyad of the clinical model. It is a form of "solidarity care" in which the formation and sustenance of a sense of community is a key feature of therapy.[25]

It is worth a note of caution, though, that projects that seek scale and widespread coverage at low cost are more effective at treating the average case than dealing with complex or more serious mental health issues. There is, of course, a potential trade-off. That said, given that mental health is increasingly considered a societal challenge on a much larger scale than in the past (and certainly before the COVID-19 pandemic), it is worth exploring strategies that can reach a large number of people—particularly those who previously

23 See https://wellbeingtrust.org.
24 See https://bha.health.maryland.gov/pages/Index.aspx.
25 See www.visiblehandscollaborative.org.

have not had access—in new ways. This could help catch the problem in its early stages rather than wait until more extensive and medically intense treatment is necessary.

Private-Public Partnerships

There is a strong link between despair and the labor market. Our incomes and wealth have been unevenly distributed across the socioeconomic spectrum, and increasingly so over time. To address despair, we must focus on better jobs, which requires collaboration with the private sector. There are examples of companies investing in job-training programs in their neighborhoods and experimenting with more equitable ownership structures, as well as government programs channeling credit and providing training to business owners in deprived areas. Yet these programs are often limited in scope and disconnected from federal public health programs.

On the other hand, several new public-private partnerships suggest a promising path. These include concepts of well-being as a frame and interventions driven by well-being data. The public sector can contribute to this area by generating national-level well-being data and including worker well-being in labor market policies. Much of the private sector has caught on to the evidence from many studies that workers with higher levels of well-being are more productive.

Enhancing worker well-being need not be expensive; indeed, it may increase efficiency. Milena Nikolova and Femke Cnossen (2021) show that workers value autonomy and being treated with respect over an average salary increase. Being autonomous tends to lead to better performance and productivity. In addition, there are complementary strategies that are both efficient and effective. Jan-Emmanuel de Neve (2021) found that workers' most important criteria for job satisfaction during the pandemic was not salary-based, but rather having a sense of belonging at the workplace.

Other efforts, which seek to support small enterprises, particularly with firm owners from disadvantaged backgrounds, have made a big difference to the size and sustainability of the small business sector at a time when it is threatened by COVID-19 and a rapidly changing economic context. Energize Colorado, for example, provides grants to help small businesses make investments in their skills and other facets of sustainability, including their ability to change economic conditions in the context of a pandemic. One of the most cited barriers to small businesses surviving is the extent to which they can access readily available and reliable information from their local governments, both about COVID-19 restrictions and other issues related to their businesses. That is an inexpensive way to improve efficiency and can be done more broadly.

Meanwhile, one of the most important factors in small-business success was the reporting of trust, hope, and belonging. At a time when large, profit-squeezing corporations dominate more and more sectors, ranging from publishing to manufacturing to service provision, having a vibrant small-business sector, which can support local talent, creativity, employment, and civic pride, seems an important antidote.

Creativity metrics can contribute. They are part of new models of "value creation" and correlate with other well-being data. They can help us move well-being and diversity and equity from "outcomes" goals to an antecedent condition for increasing the innovation capacities of business and government; creativity, by definition, does not accept stereotypes. Certain aspects of eudaimonic well-being (purpose and meaning in life) link closely with this and are relevant to the skills acquisition necessary for labor force participation in the rapidly changing economy.

A growing body of scientific evidence links creativity to the skill groups that will be essential in future economies, such as those identified by the World Economic Forum 2025.[26] Creativity is likewise linked to many of the key mechanisms that mediate well-being in work and social contexts. Indeed, we are beginning to understand creativity not only as an internal psychological process, but as the outcome of an interaction between individuals and their environment.[27]

Further, if inclusion (as measured through proxy metrics of hope, trust, and belonging) and well-being are understood as antecedent conditions and predictive signals of workforce capacity and innovation orientation, significant progress can be made toward expanding innovation capacity.[28] It is not coincidental that the Energize Colorado initiative identified these as important factors to small-business success during the pandemic.

There is also a broader movement to include human capital in environmental, social, and governance metrics, reflecting increasing national and international interest in well-being. The World Economic Forum recently published a Human Capital Accounting Framework that aims to quantify and build human capital within large organizations that have historically struggled to do so, focusing on corporate culture, stakeholder leadership, and employee well-being. The Global Reporting Initiative recently developed the Culture of Health for Business, or COH4B, program with support from the Robert Wood Johnson Foundation. The Sustainability Accounting Standards Board has made mental health, well-being, and health-related benefits a focus in a proposed revamp of its human capital standards.

This drive includes public as well as private sector agencies. The Securities and Exchange Commission is expanding reporting requirements to include a broad set of measures

26 Kaufman and Sternberg (2019). See also http://www3.weforum.org/docs/WEF_Future_of_Jobs_2020.pdf.

27 Amabile and Pratt (2016).

28 Lister et al. (2021).

including training hours, worker productivity, and turnover and is now considering requiring human capital metric reporting. And the International Organization for Standardization has specified twenty-three core metrics—including worker productivity, health and well-being, and leadership trust—for organizations to track and report. These initiatives align with the growing public interest in well-being as an umbrella objective that encompasses mental and physical health *and* the move to include employee satisfaction and engagement as part of our benchmarks of economic progress.

Conclusion

The challenges in this arena are daunting, particularly in the United States, which combines some of the highest levels of wealth in the world with falling levels of well-being, a crisis of premature mortality, high levels of poverty, a fragmented public health system, and a civil society that seems to be unraveling. As repeated many times in this book, there is no magic bullet. But there are many lessons that stem from the well-being literature—lessons that have been tested in successful interventions and provide insights into other policies that seek to address despair, mental health issues, and the challenges of a changing labor market.

The lessons that emerge, while novel, are also reminiscent of the economic development literature of the 1970s and 1980s. Top-down solutions do not work well; it is essential to involve the community in its own revival. Learn from new strategies that rely on social ties and other networks, professionals, and the public sector. Harness the energies of the private sector. Respect the pride and the input of the recipients of the support that is designed to improve their futures. Educate the young, support their aspirations, and provide mentorship and knowledge of how to prepare themselves for their futures.

And, back to the book's theme, hope matters and is part of these approaches. While hope resembles optimism—as individuals believe things will get better—an equally important part of hope (and not optimism) is that individuals can do things that improve their lives and thereby demonstrate agency over their futures. Helping them form a vision of what their futures can look like will help them have hope and aspirations.

That is not what we are seeing in millions of individuals and their communities in the United States today. And the same individuals and places in despair are passing it on to their children. As such, we need to think about how to revive entire communities and the individuals within them and then devise strategies to help the next generation not end up in the same state. The last goal is perhaps the priority, but it will be difficult to achieve without addressing the other two. Some communities will never come back, and the best we can do is encourage their youths to move away and find lives elsewhere. At the same time, many communities can come back and benefit from the kinds of strategies described above, which will provide the next generation with the option of being part of their community's revival.

As my coauthors and I recommend in our Brookings report on despair and economic recovery, there is an important role for public policy in providing logistical support—most importantly by conveying the lessons and strategies that can be adapted to other communities. Indeed, what is often missing in local efforts to turn things around is reliable information about other efforts and experiences that have succeeded and how or if they can be replicated elsewhere. This is a simple and critical role the federal government can play.

In addition, small grants to support promising efforts would also help and would be cost-effective compared to many of the more expensive support policies that are currently in place but tend to operate in silos (economic recovery efforts, for example, rarely include addressing mental health issues). Supporting mentorship programs and encouraging the private sector to provide training and internship opportunities is critical to filling the information gaps faced by the young in deprived communities. Involving community-level actors benefits both the individuals who receive support and the communities themselves, creating new agency and opportunities for change.

It is a gradual process; it will not work every time and in every place; it may even backfire. Yet without addressing our societal crisis of despair—which requires reviving hope—all our other efforts, such as reviving the economy, healing civil society, and narrowing the divides in our discourse and our politics, will not bridge the divide between those with hope and those in despair. And, in the end, if enough of society is in despair, it will make restoring hope impossible. We have some tools, albeit relatively new and imperfect ones, but they have proven effective in many places. If we do not try, we surely will not succeed.

Given that the objective of enhancing well-being can be shared across individuals, across public and private sectors, and across populations and places, it is a valuable public good. A society with higher levels of well-being has more potential to have a productive, prosperous, and democratic future. Aiming for that as an objective is surely better than the precipice the United States is presently facing.

CHAPTER 6

Can We Restore Hope in America?

"The truth is, hope isn't a promise we give. It's a promise we live."

—Amanda Gorman, the *New York Times*, January 20, 2022

I spent much of this book making the case for why hope matters today more than ever in our recent history. Why hope is critical to the next generation and why the next generation is critical to restoring the United States to a healthy civic society, a viable democracy, and a country where prosperity is not only for the privileged. This requires better understanding the roots of hope and resilience, measuring its patterns across populations and places, learning what we can about how to restore hope among populations where it has been lost, and incorporating that into our policies to improve our society's health and well-being. We have a long way to go.

As we face a crisis of confidence and identity of a historic nature, we have a chance to implement change: in the way we think of prosperity, in the way our democracy functions, in the way we educate our young, and in the way we conceive of our society's future. We still need markets and democracy as a basis; they have served us well in the past, despite working better some times than others. As Winston Churchill said, "Democracy is the worst form of government except all others that have been tried." And having spent a lot of my career studying the costs—particularly to the poor—of markets distorted by bad policies, I am also convinced—as are most economists—that we cannot do without them, although we surely can improve their functioning.

Yet for markets and democracy to function for all society, we need the majority in our society to have hope and agency, which is hardly the case now. That entails educating all of our youth (not just those who can pay for it) for tomorrow's world; we need to take care of the health and well-being of all society; and we need to restore hope and a vision for the future among those who have lost it, particularly the young. Indeed, with dysfunctional politics and labor markets with fewer opportunities for those who do not have higher levels of education, coupled with a historic pandemic, we have seen increases in depression, anxiety, and a lack of confidence in the future for the young in most places, and certainly in the United States.[1] Having a vision of a common and better future is part of the solution.

Several chapters of this book have shown different visions of the future—not just in the same country but in the same county. Populations that are equally deprived have different levels of hope, well-being, and aspirations for the future. Minorities who have been traditionally discriminated against (and still are) have made progress against all odds and still see a better future; they also see the importance of investing in skills and education.

Blue-collar whites, who essentially had privileged access to the American Dream in the past, have fallen behind and lost their life narrative and do not have one to replace it—or even one to envision. Despair rather than hope for the future is the current narrative and is being passed on to the next generation. And, equally worrisome, many in this cohort

---

1 The extent to which they have increased, though, depends on the survey, its questions, and its reference period. We discuss this in detail in Dobson et al. (forthcoming).

have also lost faith in the tools that can get them, and society in general, ahead: education, science, participation in civil society, and consensus on truth.

There is a lot we do not know about how to solve this problem. Better education and training for the young, new kinds of jobs, civic education, and other policies and programs come to mind and have been suggested by many others. They are important but they will take time. And they will not be taken up if people do not have hope in their own futures and trust in the system. In the short term, reducing despair and reviving hope is a critical part of the solution.

We can learn from well-being science. Hope has, until recently, been treated as part of happiness and other dimensions of well-being, such as eudaimonia (purpose and meaning in life), but it has not been identified as a distinct dimension with causal properties of its own. Yet many of the positive properties of well-being—better health, longevity, and resilience—have more to do with hope and its agentic properties than with momentary happiness or with the most widely used assessment of well-being—life satisfaction— which is an evaluative measure. Hope is, in the end, a more active, future-oriented dimension of well-being, while both hedonic and evaluative well-being tend to be ex post assessments rather than future-oriented ones.

This also speaks to the need to refine the definition of hope and to measure it more regularly. We need to increase our understanding of hope if we want to restore it in populations and places where it has been lost. One reason the science of well-being has advanced so much is that many measures of well-being are now included in large-scale surveys, allowing economists and other scholars to explore both its determinants and its causal properties. Yet we are just starting to measure hope and understand its correlates and causal properties.

As I have argued, it is time to do so and to think of hope in policy terms. We have a robust science to build from and an increasing interest in well-being metrics as part of our policy design and evaluation. While much of the official survey effort in the United States has been to measure the markers of ill-being, such as anxiety and depression, it is equally important to understand the positive dimensions of well-being—hope, in particular—and how/if we can use the findings to combat despair and ill-being.

This is, indeed, uncharted ground. Yet it is also a moment when unprecedented challenges to our health, social ties, jobs, and ways of living are testing our confidence in the future. Due to the pandemic, much of what we took for granted is now out of reach, such as work and school as they used to be, social ties and friendships that involved human contact, and partic-ipation in the arts and music as part of daily life. The future is even more uncertain for those who were already disadvantaged before the pandemic hit, especially the poor—and the poor in poor countries even more so. Restoring hope will be an im-portant part of navigating the future successfully.

This is not the first time we have experienced uncertainly and setbacks that have challenged our sense of the future. We had the Gilded Age followed by the Great Depression and then a new vision of a common future in the New Deal. We had the war on poverty and the civil rights movement, and then the swing back to raw individualism, trickle-down economics, and the related skepticism of government. In the late 1980s, we seemed to reach a modicum of consensus on the need to maintain a liberal, open economic system coupled with a concern for welfare, human rights, and de-mocracy at home and abroad, yet that was eroded by the 2009 financial crisis. Since then, we have lost consensus on the path forward.

The old GOP of the Gilded Age that espoused low taxes and rugged individualism now seeks as its base the disgruntled white working class. The only way it can remain competitive with this strategy seems to be to curb electoral competition. The traditional Democratic Party of the working class finds itself losing this base; it has become the party of urban elites, including the wealthy founders of technology companies. It also has become much more diverse than the GOP: it is the party of the young, minorities, and women. It is also the party of free trade (grudgingly), progressive social policies, and addressing environmental challenges. In contrast, the GOP supports the right to refuse vaccines that stop pandemics, to deny science, and to reduce an already fractured health insurance system. At the same time it is taking away women's rights to control their own bodies. Unfortunately—and at a time when most people simply want a clear and inclusive vision—many Democratic leaders are caught up in visceral battles over cancel culture and identity politics.

We need a new vision of the future, and that requires hope. It is time to prioritize society's well-being, health, and its economic prosperity. This does not mean throwing out the baby with the bath water. We have tools we did not have in the past, tools that allow us to quantify and address problems, assess how they tax our peace and prosperity, and how they hurt the mental and physical health of society, both young and old.

We are the only rich country in the world where life expectancy has declined over the past decade, driven largely by preventable deaths. The same country that produced key innovations in human progress, like the lightbulb, the airplane, and myriad treatments for diseases such as cancer and polio cannot address a problem of middle-aged death due to drug overdose and suicide. This is particularly ironic, as we have strategies and cures to improve brain health and the brain capital of our society; methodologies for incorporating human emotions and behavior into formerly static economic models; and new ways of measuring how individual interactions can aggregate into unexpected outcomes, whether it's bad—with violent tipping points—or good—with increased trust in laws and institutions.[2]

As a result, social science has developed a great deal in terms of method and precision and can now not only incorporate the approaches often used by the physical and biological sciences but also contribute to them. Among these advances is the new science of well-being measurement, which incorporates the tools and approaches of both. It has tentacles in many novel approaches, such as investing in brain health and brain capital, addressing previously ignored mental health issues, and helping to understand the interactions between genes and the environment.[3]

Well-being science can shed new light on old problems—such as poverty and despair—with new tools and with interdisciplinary collaboration between economists, psychologists, geneticists, and psychiatrists. It can also identify novel areas of research, such as why individuals with low genetic well-being endowments behave differently—and often have different reward structures—than those with higher ones, and why and how higher levels of well-being are linked to longer and more prosperous lives. Experimental research is exploring how well-being levels can increase based on this interaction, and how or if the behaviors exhibited by those with higher levels of well-being can be learned or transferred. Like any other science, there are questions we cannot yet answer and there are some biases in our instruments. Still, these tools can contribute to solutions at this critical moment.

---

2 For an excellent introduction to the formation and evolution of social norms, see Young (1998).

3 The concept of Brain Capital, which was developed by Dr. Harris Eyre of the Prodeo Brain Institute and Professor William Hayes of Oxford University, is now being operationalized as an official OECD international initiative—in large part due to their efforts. For details on it and its links to well-being, see Eyre et al. (2021).

Early in the book, I briefly reviewed the state of the art in well-being measurement, something I am proud of contributing to over the past two decades. Well-being in economics, my field, for example, has gone from the far fringes to the mainstream. Governments in the U.K., New Zealand, and now Canada are framing societal well-being as a public policy priority. While the United States lags far behind, the COVID-19 pandemic—and its toll on mental health—on top of our preexisting crisis of despair has woken us up to the need to prioritize society's well-being and economic prosperity. That gives us a chance to measure and explore the properties of a new dimension of well-being—hope—that may help us reduce the despair that afflicts much of our society.

I have spent much of this book highlighting the role of hope—and its agentic properties—in helping individuals, communities, and societies in crafting a vision for their futures. We need to further our understanding of hope to have a more concrete sense of the role it can play. One first step is to begin to measure hope in our standard well-being surveys, so scholars can explore its seeming causal properties with robust methods—once the data is available—and to include the findings in public policy discussions. We have a window of opportunity following the challenges of COVID-19 to give momentum to the need to collect the requisite data.

More difficult is our need to restore opportunities for a broad portion of society—a shift from our society's winner-take-all model. Embracing these opportunities will require rebuilding confidence and trust in the system. This will entail instilling hope in those who have lost it: hope that the system *can* work, that they can get ahead if they invest in their futures, and that communities and institutions (formal and informal) can help them.

This is important for the next generation—and particularly those who are starting at a disadvantage—who face uncertainties in labor markets, health, and social life. Hope is particularly important in contexts of deprivation and of uncertainty, as without hope people are unlikely to make the investments that will help them navigate uncertainties and take up the opportunities that eventually become available. The unknown waters we are entering compel us to experiment with change and new strategies. The system as we know it is failing. We are increasingly divided—as a society, a country, and a global community—and there is much room for new thinking and approaches.

Prioritizing human well-being instead of economic progress in our vision could be the glue that puts us back together. As noted above, this does not imply costs to our economy; ultimately, it should benefit our economic potential. We need markets, economic progress, and income-generating activities to achieve many objectives, such as improving the health, education, and well-being of our society. While how to achieve that is a subject for another book, the point is that focusing on well-being is not a zero-sum choice in terms of economic progress: populations and societies with higher levels of well-being tend to be more productive.

Yet we cannot expect a population that is divided in opportunity, education, health, and hope to be productive and cohesive. As I noted, the same country that encouraged innovations such as the lightbulb, the airplane, treatments for cancer, and the iPhone, and for a long time was considered the world's most prosperous democracy, now has large segments of its population living in despair, with no hope for today or tomorrow, no faith in science and education, and no vision of a better life for its own children. This coexists with remarkable levels of hope and resilience among some populations—the minorities who are more materially deprived and have been traditionally discriminated against. It is not easy to merge these visions.

One means to bring them closer together is to enhance the hope of those who do not have it and to highlight avenues toward a better future. As discussed in chapter 5, we have some examples, experiences, and experiments in the well-being field to look to, as well as some from other approaches and disciplines. The first step is to address the widespread despair of large numbers people—of all ages and stages. A second step, which is important for the young, is providing mentorship on what the future can bring for the next generation, what opportunities there are, and what skills are necessary to participate in them.

One thing we can—and must—do is support the aspirations of those who do have them. In this case, those adolescents with higher education for the most part seem to have mentors—either in their families or within their communities. Yet they will still need help along the way, ranging from information about how to train and what skills they will need, to logistics and financial support. That is the easy first step. Yet their succeeding will, perhaps, convince those who do not have hope and aspirations that it is worth trying. At the least, we should extend knowledge to them about what they can achieve if they invest in their own training.

This is uncharted territory. Rarely have whites taken lessons from the minorities they traditionally discriminated against. What to do? In part, perhaps just showing them the trends and the changes—such minorities narrowing the disparities in health and education and other outcomes—may have a role (although of course it also might backfire in the current context of increasing racism).

Still, changing the narrative by creating a positive one may be an important step. It is no surprise that if low-income white adolescents have little support for their aspirations, have no faith in higher education and science, and have low trust in others, their vision for the future is limited to what they have and know. That is not only sad on its own, it is also unlikely that, in the changing labor markets, they can even do as well as their parents. Without acquiring more skills and

credentials, they are unlikely to have stable jobs, health insurance, and other markers that help establish a sustainable
and better future. They will end up navigating the constant
uncertainty that makes it difficult to plan or save for the future.

Hope may seem like a pipe dream. Yet precisely because
it includes the will to make things better as well as believing
they can be, it is a critical step. Many programs, as described
in chapter 5, have some relevant lessons. If restoring community spirit and solidarity with the objective of helping youths
get ahead is an objective, programs like Portland Community
Squash and the What Works Centre for Wellbeing come to
mind, in part because they break down existing barriers—
including racial ones—that hold back particular groups. In
this case, low-income whites may need as much if not more
support than minorities, at least in in terms of developing a
new narrative that includes building for and investing in a
better future.

Mental health, though, is becoming a pressing issue for
teens and young adults, in part due to the uncertainty that
COVID-19 created and due to ongoing trends, such as the decline in low-skill jobs. Mental health issues early in life can be
a lifelong barrier to success if they are not diagnosed early. The
increasing calls for screening in schools and as part of primary
care are a key preventive approach. So is making care widely
available to those who need it and introducing it into the public
discourse in a way that is not stigmatizing.[4]

None of these solutions are complete or certain—indeed,
they are just initial steps toward tackling a complex social

4 Data from the Gallup World Poll, for example, finds that women report
higher levels of life satisfaction than men but higher levels of stress and depression. While on the one hand the higher life satisfaction scores are in part due
to reporting bias and low expectations of women in very poor countries. The
lower levels of depression reported by men likely also suffer from bias, as men
are more likely to feel stigma in discussing mental health, particularly in poor
contexts where it is not the norm. See Montgomery (2022).

problem that entails public and mental health, psychology, education, and labor markets (and, of course, hope for the future). Yet without restoring hope and related aspirations as a starting point, it is unlikely that any solution will work; we would likely have another generation in despair. Perhaps, though, the Jamils and Davilas and Antoines will be working hand in hand with the Taylors and Devins and Dariuses at good jobs with bright futures. It is a vision we can strive for—and we may even help them achieve it—by restoring hope.

Statistical Analysis

Model 1

In the first model we specify a lagged model as follows:

$$Outcomes_{i,wave2} = \beta_0 + \beta_1 Aspirations_{i,wave1} + X_{i,wave1} \Gamma + \varepsilon_{i,wave2}$$

Where $Outcomes_{i,wave2}$ include the following outcomes: school attainment, enrollment status, share of time dedicated to school-related activities, professional development training, or risky behaviors. $Aspirations_{i,wave1}$ include each of the three types of aspirations (education, occupation, or migration), and $X_{i,wave1}$ is a vector of time-varying controls, including individual- and household-level characteristics and personality traits. Finally, ε_{it} is an unobserved error term. This set-up allows us to carry out simple tests to measure the correlation between aspirations and future outcomes. If there is no correlation, we would expect β_1 to be insignificant.

Model 2

We specify the second model as follows:

$$\Delta Outcomes_{i,w2-w1} = \beta_1 \Delta Aspirations_{i,w2-w1} + \Delta X_{i,w2-w1} \Gamma + \Delta \varepsilon_{i,w2-w1}$$

Thus, we explore how changes in aspirations *within* individuals are associated with changes in human capital outcomes between Wave 1 and Wave 2. Like Model 1, our parameter of interest is β_1.

Table A.1. Testing Nonrandom Attrition across Observables

	Lost to follow-up	Followed up	t-statistic	p-value
Individual characteristics				
Female	42%	57%	−2.6	0.01**
Age of child (in years)	18.44	18.45	−0.1	0.90
Married	5%	5%	0.2	0.87
Any children	12%	13%	−0.2	0.81
Deceased parent	5%	9%	−1.5	0.13
Worked in the past 12 months	79%	76%	0.6	0.53
Currently employed	42%	33%	1.7	0.10
Subjective relative income (0–6 score)	2.90	2.98	−1.2	0.22
Aspirations				
Educational (0–10 score)	7.00	7.75	−2.5	0.01*
Occupational (0–10 score)	7.97	8.07	−0.5	0.62
Migration (0–10 score)	5.34	5.03	0.7	0.46
Personality traits				
Emotional symptoms (0–10 score)	3.67	4.16	−1.7	0.10
Internal locus of control (0–6 score)	3.21	3.24	−0.3	0.75
External locus of control (0–6 score)	2.53	2.49	0.3	0.75
Self-efficacy (0–15 score)	10.27	9.96	1.5	0.14
Subjective well-being (0–8 score)	4.70	4.69	0.0	0.97
Outcomes				
Average years of education	11.7	11.8	−0.6	0.55
Enrolled full-time	60%	71%	−2.0	0.05*
Share of time spent on school-related activities	34%	40%	−2.0	0.05*
Pursue any professional development activities	33%	43%	−1.7	0.09
Smokes cigarettes	47%	41%	1.1	0.29
Drinks alcohol	64%	68%	−0.7	0.50
Risky sex	21%	17%	0.8	0.45
Carries weapon	2%	3%	−0.6	0.56

Note: We rescaled the three types of aspirations on a ten-point scale to make it easier to compare the average level of aspirations across all three types. All individual characteristics except age and subjective relative income are dummy variables. All outcomes except average years of education and share of time spent on school-related activities are dummy variables. The remaining variables are scores, with the range shown in brackets. P-value is from two-tailed t-test. The stars represent statistical significance as follows: * $p < 0.05$, ** $p < 0.01$, *** $p < 0.001$.

Table A.2. Changes in Average Aspirations over Time

Aspirations	Wave 1	Wave 2	p-value
Education	7.8 (SD 2.3)	7.5 (SD 2.6)	0.09
Occupation	8.1 (SD 1.7)	8.1 (SD 1.9)	0.74
Migration	5.0 (SD 3.3)	4.9 (SD 3.4)	0.81

Note: We rescaled the three types of aspirations on a ten-point scale to make it easier to compare across all three types of aspirations. P-value is from two-tailed t-test. The stars represent statistical significance as follows: * $p < 0.05$, ** $p < 0.01$, *** $p < 0.001$.

Table A.3. Personality Traits over Time

	Wave 1 (n = 400)	Wave 2 (n = 301)	t-test p-value
Emotional symptoms (0–10 score)	4.0	4.2	0.36
Internal locus of control (0–6 score)	3.2	4.6	0.00***
External locus of control (0–6 score)	2.5	2.5	0.65
Self-efficacy (0–15 score)	10.0	10.2	0.12
Subjective well-being (0–8 score)	4.7	4.8	0.22
Impatience	0.4	0.5	0.32
Belief in hard work	3.6	3.3	0.00***
Willingness to take risks	2.6	3.0	0.00***
Sociability	3.0	3.0	0.99
Self-esteem	3.1	3.3	0.00***
Optimism	3.4	3.6	0.00***

Note: All variables in the last six rows are dummy variables. P-value is from two-tailed t-test. The stars represent statistical significance as follows: * $p < 0.05$, ** $p < 0.01$, *** $p < 0.001$, * $p < 0.05$, ** $p < 0.01$, *** $p < 0.001$.

Table A.4. Human Capital Outcomes over Time

	Wave 1 (n = 400)	Wave 2 (n = 301)	t-statistic	p-value
Average years of education	11.8	14.3	−15.2	0.00***
Enrolled full-time	68%	50%	4.8	0.00***
Share of time spent on school-related activities	39%	28%	4.6	0.00***
Pursue any professional development activities	41%	55%	−4.0	0.20
Smokes cigarettes	42%	49%	−1.7	0.09
Drinks alcohol	67%	81%	−4.3	0.00***
Risky sex	18%	31%	−3.8	0.00***
Carries weapon	3%	2%	0.4	0.72

Note: All outcomes except average years of education are dummy variables. P-value is from two-tailed t-test. The stars represent statistical significance as follows: * $p < 0.05$, ** $p < 0.01$, *** $p < 0.001$.

Table A.5.1. Model 1 (Lagged Model). Educational Aspirations

Variables	Average years of education	Enrolled full-time	Share of time spent on school activities	Pursue any professional development activities	Smokes cigarettes	Drinks alcohol	Risky sex	Carries weapon
Educational aspirations at Wave 1	0.25**	0.27***	0.30***	0.14*	-0.14*	-0.03	-0.19**	0.03
	(0.09)	(0.06)	(0.06)	(0.07)	(0.06)	(0.05)	(0.07)	(0.04)
Female	0.01	-0.11	-0.18**	-0.06	-0.30***	-0.12*	-0.11	-0.08
	(0.06)	(0.06)	(0.06)	(0.06)	(0.06)	(0.05)	(0.07)	(0.05)
Household asset index	0.16**	0.25***	0.25***	0.03	0.02	0.01	-0.16*	-0.05
	(0.06)	(0.05)	(0.05)	(0.06)	(0.06)	(0.04)	(0.07)	(0.07)
Total shocks experienced	0.02	-0.05	-0.10	0.05	0.01	0.04	0.01	-0.03
	(0.06)	(0.06)	(0.06)	(0.06)	(0.06)	(0.04)	(0.07)	(0.03)
Emotional symptoms	0.22**	0.22***	0.20***	0.09	0.07	0.06	0.06	0.05
	(0.07)	(0.06)	(0.06)	(0.06)	(0.06)	(0.05)	(0.07)	(0.06)
Internal locus of control	0.01	-0.04	-0.03	-0.03	0.18*	0.05	0.15	0.14
	(0.07)	(0.08)	(0.09)	(0.09)	(0.09)	(0.07)	(0.09)	(0.08)
External locus of control	-0.03	-0.03	-0.02	-0.04	-0.08	0.00	-0.09	-0.19*
	(0.06)	(0.07)	(0.06)	(0.07)	(0.06)	(0.05)	(0.07)	(0.09)
Self-efficacy	0.05	0.04	0.04	-0.03	0.02	0.04	-0.02	0.01
	(0.05)	(0.06)	(0.06)	(0.06)	(0.07)	(0.04)	(0.07)	(0.07)
Subjective well-being	0.04	0.02	0.03	-0.05	-0.03	0.05	-0.04	-0.02
	(0.06)	(0.05)	(0.05)	(0.06)	(0.06)	(0.05)	(0.07)	(0.05)
Impatience	-0.06	-0.06	-0.03	0.05	-0.04	-0.10*	-0.07	-0.08
	(0.06)	(0.06)	(0.06)	(0.06)	(0.06)	(0.04)	(0.07)	(0.05)
Belief in hard work	-0.01	0.02	-0.00	0.05	0.01	-0.01	0.11	0.07
	(0.05)	(0.07)	(0.06)	(0.06)	(0.05)	(0.07)	(0.07)	(0.05)
Constant	0.57***	-0.24**	-0.20**	0.11	0.18*	-0.10	0.23**	0.05
	(0.07)	(0.07)	(0.07)	(0.08)	(0.09)	(0.06)	(0.09)	(0.09)
Observations	248	300	301	301	297	296	291	296
R-squared	0.16	0.20	0.23	0.04	0.11	0.06	0.07	0.05

Note: We applied robust standard errors (in paretheses) and standardized the coefficients using the whole sample's standard deviation. The stars represent statistical significance as follows: * $p < 0.05$, ** $p < 0.01$, *** $p < 0.001$.

Table A.5.2. Model 1 (Lagged model). Occupational Aspirations

Variables	Average years of education	Enrolled full-time	Share of time spent on school activities	Pursue any professional development activities	Smokes cigarettes	Drinks alcohol	Risky sex	Carries weapon
Occupational aspirations at Wave 1	0.12*	0.12*	0.16**	0.01	-0.04	-0.10	-0.11	0.02
	(0.05)	(0.06)	(0.05)	(0.06)	(0.05)	(0.06)	(0.07)	(0.02)
Female	-0.02	-0.14*	-0.22***	-0.07	-0.29***	-0.10*	-0.09	-0.09
	(0.06)	(0.06)	(0.06)	(0.06)	(0.06)	(0.05)	(0.07)	(0.05)
Household asset index	0.20**	0.30***	0.31***	0.05	-0.01	-0.01	-0.20**	-0.05
	(0.06)	(0.05)	(0.05)	(0.06)	(0.06)	(0.04)	(0.07)	(0.07)
Total shocks experienced	0.05	-0.04	-0.09	0.05	-0.01	0.03	0.00	-0.03
	(0.06)	(0.06)	(0.06)	(0.06)	(0.06)	(0.04)	(0.07)	(0.03)
Emotional symptoms	0.21**	0.21***	0.19**	0.09	0.08	0.06	0.06	0.05
	(0.07)	(0.06)	(0.06)	(0.06)	(0.06)	(0.05)	(0.07)	(0.06)
Internal locus of control	0.01	-0.05	-0.05	-0.03	0.20*	0.07	0.16	0.14
	(0.07)	(0.09)	(0.09)	(0.09)	(0.09)	(0.07)	(0.09)	(0.08)
External locus of control	-0.03	-0.03	-0.02	-0.05	-0.08	-0.00	-0.09	-0.19*
	(0.06)	(0.07)	(0.07)	(0.07)	(0.07)	(0.05)	(0.07)	(0.09)
Self-efficacy	0.07	0.06	0.07	-0.03	0.00	0.04	-0.03	0.01
	(0.05)	(0.06)	(0.06)	(0.06)	(0.07)	(0.04)	(0.07)	(0.07)
Subjective well-being	0.05	0.04	0.05	-0.04	-0.04	0.04	-0.04	-0.02
	(0.07)	(0.06)	(0.05)	(0.06)	(0.06)	(0.05)	(0.07)	(0.05)
Impatience	-0.07	-0.07	-0.04	0.04	-0.02	-0.11**	-0.05	-0.08
	(0.06)	(0.06)	(0.06)	(0.06)	(0.06)	(0.04)	(0.07)	(0.05)
Belief in hard work	-0.02	0.02	0.00	0.06	0.00	0.00	0.12	0.07
	(0.06)	(0.07)	(0.06)	(0.07)	(0.05)	(0.07)	(0.07)	(0.05)
Constant	0.62***	-0.22**	-0.18*	0.12	0.18*	-0.10	0.22*	0.05
	(0.07)	(0.08)	(0.08)	(0.08)	(0.09)	(0.06)	(0.09)	(0.09)
Observations	245	297	298	298	295	294	289	294
R-squared	0.13	0.16	0.19	0.02	0.09	0.07	0.06	0.05

Note: We applied robust standard errors (in paretheses) and standardized the coefficients using the whole sample's standard deviation. The stars represent statistical significance as follows: * p < 0.05, ** p < 0.01, *** p < 0.001.

Table A.5.3. Model 1 (Lagged Model). Migration Aspirations

Variables	Average years of education	Enrolled full-time	Share of time spent on school activities	Pursue any professional development activities	Smokes cigarettes	Drinks alcohol	Risky sex	Carries weapon
Migration aspirations at Wave 1	0.04	0.03	0.02	0.13*	-0.05	-0.07	-0.08	-0.10*
	(0.06)	(0.06)	(0.06)	(0.1)	(0.06)	(0.05)	(0.07)	(0.05)
Female	0.02	-0.12	-0.19**	-0.07	-0.29***	-0.13*	-0.10	-0.11*
	(0.07)	(0.06)	(0.07)	(0.1)	(0.07)	(0.06)	(0.07)	(0.06)
Household asset index	0.21**	0.30***	0.31***	0.07	0.00	-0.02	-0.22**	-0.07
	(0.07)	(0.05)	(0.05)	(0.1)	(0.06)	(0.05)	(0.07)	(0.07)
Total shocks experienced	0.06	0.00	-0.03	0.07	-0.00	0.04	-0.04	-0.05
	(0.07)	(0.06)	(0.06)	(0.1)	(0.07)	(0.05)	(0.07)	(0.04)
Emotional symptoms	0.21**	0.22**	0.17**	0.04	0.06	0.06	0.11	0.00
	(0.08)	(0.07)	(0.06)	(0.1)	(0.07)	(0.06)	(0.08)	(0.05)
Internal locus of control	0.03	-0.04	-0.05	-0.01	0.20*	0.06	0.24**	0.15
	(0.08)	(0.09)	(0.09)	(0.1)	(0.10)	(0.07)	(0.09)	(0.08)
External locus of control	0.01	-0.06	-0.05	-0.07	-0.10	-0.02	-0.11	-0.16
	(0.06)	(0.07)	(0.07)	(0.1)	(0.07)	(0.05)	(0.08)	(0.08)
Self-efficacy	0.04	0.07	0.06	-0.07	0.02	0.05	-0.03	0.05
	(0.05)	(0.06)	(0.06)	(0.1)	(0.07)	(0.04)	(0.07)	(0.07)
Subjective well-being	0.05	0.05	0.07	-0.02	-0.01	0.05	-0.05	-0.08
	(0.07)	(0.06)	(0.06)	(0.1)	(0.07)	(0.05)	(0.08)	(0.04)
Impatience	-0.08	-0.07	-0.05	-0.00	-0.04	-0.13**	-0.08	-0.12*
	(0.06)	(0.06)	(0.06)	(0.1)	(0.06)	(0.04)	(0.07)	(0.05)
Belief in hard work	-0.01	0.02	0.00	0.10	0.00	0.01	0.10	0.05
	(0.06)	(0.07)	(0.06)	(0.1)	(0.06)	(0.08)	(0.07)	(0.04)
Constant	0.64***	-0.21*	-0.18*	0.10	0.22*	-0.09	0.33***	0.05
	(0.08)	(0.08)	(0.08)	(0.1)	(0.10)	(0.07)	(0.10)	(0.10)
Observations	217	265	266	266	263	262	258	262
R-squared	0.12	0.16	0.17	0.04	0.10	0.08	0.08	0.09

Note: We applied robust standard errors (in paretheses) and standardized the coefficients using the whole sample's standard deviation. The stars represent statistical significance as follows: * p < 0.05, ** p < 0.01, *** p < 0.001.

Table A.6.1. Model 2 (Individual Fixed Effects Model). Educational Aspirations

Variables	Average years of education	Enrolled full-time	Share of time spent on school activities	Pursue any professional development activities	Smokes cigarettes	Drinks alcohol	Risky sex	Carries weapon
Educational aspirations	0.08	0.26***	0.21***	-0.07	-0.05	0.07	-0.00	-0.14*
	(0.06)	(0.06)	(0.05)	(0.06)	(0.06)	(0.06)	(0.07)	(0.07)
Marital status	0.02	-0.17***	-0.14***	-0.04	-0.05	-0.08	0.15*	-0.13
	(0.05)	(0.04)	(0.04)	(0.06)	(0.05)	(0.04)	(0.06)	(0.07)
Employment	0.05	-0.12*	-0.27***	0.16**	0.03	0.00	0.01	-0.10
	(0.05)	(0.05)	(0.04)	(0.06)	(0.04)	(0.05)	(0.06)	(0.06)
Total shocks experienced	-0.20***	0.10	0.03	0.03	-0.05	0.05	-0.03	0.02
	(0.06)	(0.06)	(0.05)	(0.07)	(0.05)	(0.06)	(0.06)	(0.04)
Emotional symptoms	-0.05	-0.03	-0.06	0.03	-0.05	-0.01	0.11	0.10
	(0.07)	(0.07)	(0.06)	(0.08)	(0.07)	(0.07)	(0.09)	(0.08)
Internal locus of control	0.32***	-0.07	-0.05	0.04	0.06	0.02	0.11*	-0.02
	(0.04)	(0.04)	(0.04)	(0.05)	(0.04)	(0.05)	(0.05)	(0.04)
External locus of control	0.01	0.01	0.02	0.05	0.07	0.02	-0.00	0.13
	(0.05)	(0.06)	(0.05)	(0.06)	(0.04)	(0.05)	(0.05)	(0.08)
Self-efficacy	0.02	-0.09	-0.11*	0.13*	-0.05	-0.04	0.01	0.01
	(0.05)	(0.05)	(0.05)	(0.06)	(0.05)	(0.06)	(0.07)	(0.07)
Subjective well-being	0.01	0.12*	0.08	0.14*	-0.03	-0.07	-0.01	0.10
	(0.06)	(0.06)	(0.05)	(0.06)	(0.05)	(0.06)	(0.06)	(0.06)
Impatience	-0.03	0.07	0.10*	-0.08	0.05	0.07	0.03	0.06
	(0.05)	(0.05)	(0.04)	(0.05)	(0.05)	(0.05)	(0.05)	(0.07)
Belief in hard work	-0.20***	0.03	0.07	-0.12*	-0.01	0.15**	-0.06	-0.02
	(0.05)	(0.06)	(0.05)	(0.06)	(0.04)	(0.06)	(0.06)	(0.05)
Constant	0.02***	-0.00	0.00***	-0.00***	0.00	0.00	-0.00	-0.00
	(0.00)	(0.00)	(0.00)	(0.00)	(0.00)	(0.00)	(0.00)	(0.00)
Observations	645	700	701	701	688	676	678	688
R-squared	0.43	0.20	0.26	0.10	0.04	0.06	0.10	0.07
Participants	397	400	400	400	398	395	395	399

Note: We applied robust standard errors (in parentheses) and standardized the coefficients using the whole sample's standard deviation. The stars represent statistical significance as follows: * $p < 0.05$, ** $p < 0.01$, *** $p < 0.001$.

Table A.6.2. Model 2 (Individual Fixed Effects Model). Occupational Aspirations

Variables	Average years of education	Enrolled full-time	Share of time spent on school activities	Pursue any professional development activities	Smokes cigarettes	Drinks alcohol	Risky sex	Carries weapon
Occupational aspirations	0.01	0.08	0.03	-0.04	-0.18**	-0.07	-0.02	-0.13
	(0.05)	(0.07)	(0.05)	(0.06)	(0.06)	(0.07)	(0.08)	(0.07)
Marital status	0.02	-0.15**	-0.12*	-0.05	-0.04	-0.05	0.16*	-0.17
	(0.06)	(0.06)	(0.05)	(0.07)	(0.06)	(0.05)	(0.07)	(0.10)
Employment	0.04	-0.08	-0.24***	0.16*	0.02	-0.02	0.04	-0.08
	(0.06)	(0.06)	(0.05)	(0.07)	(0.04)	(0.06)	(0.06)	(0.07)
Total shocks experienced	-0.22***	0.05	-0.00	0.04	-0.04	0.08	-0.08	0.03
	(0.07)	(0.07)	(0.06)	(0.08)	(0.05)	(0.06)	(0.07)	(0.04)
Emotional symptoms	-0.13	-0.04	-0.09	-0.05	-0.01	-0.03	0.16	0.07
	(0.07)	(0.08)	(0.07)	(0.10)	(0.07)	(0.07)	(0.11)	(0.06)
Internal locus of control	0.32***	-0.11*	-0.09*	0.01	0.05	0.02	0.07	-0.00
	(0.04)	(0.05)	(0.04)	(0.06)	(0.04)	(0.05)	(0.06)	(0.05)
External locus of control	-0.04	-0.00	-0.00	0.09	0.05	-0.02	0.03	0.13
	(0.05)	(0.07)	(0.06)	(0.06)	(0.04)	(0.05)	(0.06)	(0.09)
Self-efficacy	-0.04	-0.12	-0.14**	0.13	-0.00	-0.04	0.00	-0.02
	(0.06)	(0.07)	(0.05)	(0.07)	(0.05)	(0.06)	(0.07)	(0.09)
Subjective well-being	0.00	0.13*	0.09	0.15*	-0.06	-0.09	0.03	0.07
	(0.06)	(0.06)	(0.05)	(0.07)	(0.05)	(0.06)	(0.06)	(0.06)
Impatience	-0.05	0.07	0.06	-0.05	0.06	0.05	0.04	-0.01
	(0.06)	(0.06)	(0.05)	(0.06)	(0.05)	(0.06)	(0.06)	(0.06)
Belief in hard work	-0.19**	0.06	0.05	-0.16*	-0.02	0.17**	-0.07	0.00
	(0.07)	(0.06)	(0.05)	(0.06)	(0.04)	(0.06)	(0.06)	(0.06)
Constant	0.02***	0.02***	0.02***	-0.02***	-0.01***	-0.00	-0.01	-0.01*
	(0.01)	(0.00)	(0.00)	(0.00)	(0.00)	(0.00)	(0.00)	(0.00)
Observations	603	645	645	645	635	623	625	635
R-squared	0.44	0.15	0.21	0.10	0.09	0.09	0.11	0.08
Participants	396	399	399	399	396	390	391	397

Note: We applied robust standard errors (in paretheses) and standardized the coefficients using the whole sample's standard deviation. The stars represent statistical significance as follows: * $p < 0.05$, ** $p < 0.01$, *** $p < 0.001$.

Table A.6.3. Model 2 (Individual Fixed Effects Model). Migration Aspirations

Variables	Average years of education	Enrolled full-time	Share of time spent on school activities	Pursue any professional development activities	Smokes cigarettes	Drinks alcohol	Risky sex	Carries weapon
Migration aspirations	0.02	0.05	0.02	-0.04	0.11	0.10	0.10	0.03
	(0.06)	(0.06)	(0.06)	(0.07)	(0.06)	(0.07)	(0.07)	(0.06)
Marital status	0.01	-0.23***	-0.22***	0.01	-0.06	-0.04	0.16*	-0.18
	(0.06)	(0.06)	(0.06)	(0.06)	(0.07)	(0.05)	(0.08)	(0.10)
Employment	0.08	-0.12	-0.28***	0.21**	0.02	-0.00	0.03	-0.12
	(0.06)	(0.07)	(0.06)	(0.07)	(0.05)	(0.06)	(0.06)	(0.07)
Total shocks experienced	-0.17*	0.03	-0.07	0.06	-0.03	0.07	0.05	0.06
	(0.07)	(0.07)	(0.06)	(0.08)	(0.06)	(0.08)	(0.08)	(0.05)
Emotional symptoms	-0.00	-0.11	-0.12	0.04	-0.04	0.01	0.00	0.12
	(0.07)	(0.09)	(0.08)	(0.09)	(0.08)	(0.08)	(0.11)	(0.12)
Internal locus of control	0.29***	-0.08	-0.09	0.00	0.09*	0.02	0.11	0.01
	(0.05)	(0.05)	(0.05)	(0.06)	(0.04)	(0.06)	(0.06)	(0.05)
External locus of control	-0.03	0.07	0.06	0.09	0.08	0.03	-0.03	0.08
	(0.06)	(0.08)	(0.06)	(0.06)	(0.06)	(0.07)	(0.07)	(0.10)
Self-efficacy	0.00	-0.01	-0.03	0.16*	-0.12*	-0.03	0.00	0.04
	(0.06)	(0.07)	(0.06)	(0.07)	(0.05)	(0.07)	(0.09)	(0.08)
Subjective well-being	0.05	0.15	0.08	0.09	-0.06	-0.02	-0.01	0.13
	(0.07)	(0.08)	(0.06)	(0.07)	(0.07)	(0.08)	(0.07)	(0.09)
Impatience	-0.08	0.06	0.09	-0.12	0.09	0.07	0.01	0.11
	(0.07)	(0.07)	(0.06)	(0.06)	(0.06)	(0.07)	(0.06)	(0.08)
Belief in hard work	-0.19**	-0.03	-0.01	-0.11	0.04	0.18**	-0.04	0.04
	(0.06)	(0.07)	(0.05)	(0.06)	(0.05)	(0.06)	(0.07)	(0.06)
Constant	-0.01	0.00	0.00	-0.02***	0.04***	0.02***	0.02***	0.01
	(0.01)	(0.00)	(0.00)	(0.00)	(0.00)	(0.00)	(0.00)	(0.00)
Observations	558	596	596	596	586	575	579	587
R-squared	0.40	0.13	0.21	0.12	0.08	0.08	0.08	0.08
Participants	379	385	385	385	381	376	379	382

Note: We applied robust standard errors (in paretheses) and standardized the coefficients using the whole sample's standard deviation. The stars represent statistical significance as follows: * p < 0.05, ** p < 0.01, *** p < 0.001.

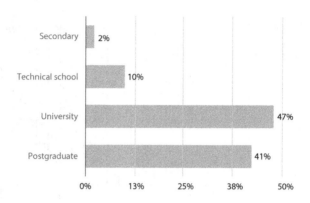

Figure A.1. Educational aspirations in Wave 1

Figure A.2. Occupational aspirations in Wave 1

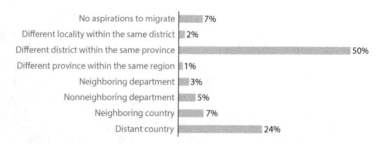

Figure A.3. Aspirations to migrate in Wave 1

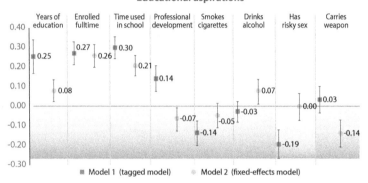

Figure A.4. Comparing coefficients between Model 1 (lagged model) and Model 2 (fixed effects model). *Note:* We standardized the coefficients using the whole sample's standard deviation. Model 1 controlled for sex, total shocks experienced, household asset index, and the following personality traits: emotional symptoms, locus of control (internal and external), self-efficacy, subjective well-being, impatience, and belief in hard work. Model 2 controlled for marital status, employment status, total shocks experienced, and the same personality traits as Model 1. The dot and square show the coefficient, and the bars the robust standard errors.

Survey—"Thinking about the Future"

THE BROOKINGS INSTITUTION AND WASHINGTON UNIVERSITY IN ST. LOUIS

Respondent Instructions and Consent Section

This survey, designed by the Brookings Institution and Washington University in St. Louis, is being fielded by the NORC survey team, which has worked for many years in this and surrounding areas. The survey is exploring the expectations for the future that young people of your age have. As the consent form below explains, the survey is entirely confidential. We will not disclose your identity, and if there is any question that you are not comfortable with, you do not have to answer it. Please fill in your responses to the questions in this form, and the members of the NORC team that are here will be available to answer any questions that you have.

Your participation will give us very important information about the problems and needs in different aspects of the life of young people like you, with a focus on your hopes and dreams for the future, and the challenges that you face in achieving them. It will take you approximately 20 to 25 minutes to fill it out.

The answers you give should be real, based on what you really think and/or do. There are no right or wrong answers. **Once again, if there is a question you do not want to answer, you can leave it blank.** If you do not understand any questions or need help, you can ask the interviewer who gave you the questionnaire.

Section 1: Household

INFORMATION ON THE RESPONDENT

Q1: Are you the head of your household? 01 = YES 02 = NO	
Q2: What is your age?	
Q3: What is your race?	
Q4: What is your gender?	
Q5: Where were you born? (City or county)	
Q6: How long have you lived in this locality?	

If you are NOT the head of the household (HoH), please answer Q1–Q2:

Q1: Who is the head of your household? 01 = Parent 02 = Partner 03 = Friend 04 = Other	
Q2: Where was he/she born? 01 = Same town/neighborhood 02 = Different locality, same county 03 = Different state 04 = Different country	

LOCATION AND HOUSEHOLD TRAITS

For each question, unless otherwise stated, 01 = YES; 02 = NO

Q1: How long have you been living in your current home? **Write down: number of months or years (please specify which).**	
Q2: Do you or someone in this household own the house, condo, or mobile home?	
Q2a: If NO to Q2, do you rent your current home?	
Q3: Do you own a car, truck, or motorcycle?	
Q4: What is the approximate value of your possessions (home, car, etc.)?	US$
Q5: Do you have any debt on these possessions?	
Q6: Do you have access to the internet in your home/on your phone?	
Q7: Do you have a computer or tablet in your home?	

PARENTAL BACKGROUND

For each question, unless otherwise stated, 01 = YES; 02 = NO

These questions are about your parents.	
Q1: Is your father alive?	
Q2: Is your mother alive?	
Q3: Was your primary caregiver one of your parents or someone else? 01 = Parent 02 = Someone else	

These questions are about the primary person who took care of you in the past.	
Q4: Is your primary caregiver still alive?	
Q5: Do you live with your parents or primary caregiver?	
If response to Q5 is YES, please skip to Q7. Otherwise, from the date you stopped living with your parent(s) or other caregiver.	
Q6: How often do you have contact with her/him/them? 01 = Daily 02 = Weekly 03 = Monthly 04 = Annually 00 = Never	
These questions are about your parents' background.	
Q7: What level of education did your mother attain? 01 = High school or less 02 = GED 03 = Some college, no degree 04 = College 05 = Technical or vocational degree 06 = Postgrad	
Q8: What level of education did your father attain? 01 = High school or less 02 = GED 03 = Some college, no degree 04 = College 05 = Technical or vocational degree 06 = Postgrad	
Q9: What is/was your mother's occupation?	
Q10: What is/was your father's occupation?	

Section 2: Subjective Well-Being

BEST POSSIBLE LIFE

These questions are about different aspects of your life. Please think of a ladder with 11 steps. Suppose the eleventh step, at the very top, represents the best possible life for you, and the bottom represents the worst possible life for you. For each question, please record step number 0–10.

Q1: Where would you place yourself today?	
Q2: Where on the ladder do you think you were 10 years ago?	
Q3: Where on the ladder do you think you will be in approximately 5 years' time?	

CESD 10

Please indicate how often you have felt this way **during the past week** by checking the appropriate box for each question.

	Rarely or none of the time (less than 1 day)	Some or a little of the time (1–2 days)	Occasionally /moderate amount of time (3–4 days)	Most or all of the time (5–7 days)
Q1: I was bothered by things that usually don't bother me.				
Q2: I had trouble keeping my mind on what I was doing.				
Q3: I felt depressed.				
Q4: I felt that everything I did was an effort.				
Q5: I felt hopeful about the future.				
Q6: I felt fearful.				
Q7: My sleep was restless.				
Q8: I was happy.				
Q9: I was lonely.				
Q10: I could not get going.				

Section 3: Education

CURRENT EDUCATION

Q1: What is your current education status? 01 = Not a student 02 = Full-time student 03 = Part-time student	
Q2: What is your highest degree of education attainment? 01 = Less than a high school degree 02 = High school degree or GED 03 = Some college but no degree 04 = Certificate or technical degree 05 = Associate's degree 06 = Bachelor's degree 07 = Some graduate or professional school	
Q3: Thinking about where you attained your highest degree, what kind of institution was that? 01 = Public 02 = Private 03 = Charter or other	

EDUCATION COSTS

Q1: In the past year, how much did you spend (approximately) on tuition, fees and other education costs such as books?	US$
Q2: How much did you spend, approximately, on additional costs, such as transportation and equipment (such as computers)?	US$
Q3: How do you finance your education? (select all that apply) 01 = Own savings 02 = Parents' savings 03 = Work and study (including Federal work-study) 04 = Loans	

Section 4: Employment, Earnings, and Time-Use

LABOR FORCE PARTICIPATION, PART 1

These questions are about your current and previous *paid and unpaid* work activities.

Q1: What best describes your current employment situation? 01 = Self-employed, full-time for pay (include contract work) 02 = Self-employed, part-time for pay (include contract work) 03 = Work full-time for pay 04 = Work part-time for pay 05 = Unemployed, looking for work 06 = Unemployed, not looking for work 07 = Disabled, not able to work 08 = Stay at home parent or spouse 09 = Full-time caregiver for a family member	
Q2: How many different jobs do you currently have? 01 = None 02 = One 03 = Two 04 = Three or more	
Q3: What are your hours worked per week, on average? 01 = None 02 = 10 or less 03 = > 10 to 20 04 = > 20 to 40 05 = > 40	
Q4: How uncertain is your work schedule each week? 01 = Very uncertain 02 = Somewhat uncertain 03 = Not at all uncertain	
Q5: Do you work in the gig economy, such as driving for Lyft/Uber; home production or services; Amazon, M-Turk, etc.? 01 = Yes, all the time 02 = Yes, sometimes 03 = No	
Q6: How do you compare that to your other work (if yes)? 01 = Pay is better (or not) 02 = Flexibility is better (or not) 03 = Other	

Q7: Can you estimate approximately how much you earn annually (gross) from your combined work activities? 01 = $5000 or less 02 = > $5000 to $15,000 03 = > $15,000 to $25,000 04 = > $25,000 to $40,000 05 = > $40,000	
Q8: Is the total income of your household greater than that of your personal earnings (listed above)?	

LABOR FORCE PARTICIPATION, PART 2

For each question, unless otherwise stated, 01 = YES; 02 = NO; 03 = OTHER

Q1: At any point in the last 12 months were you unemployed?	
Q2: During the time you were without work in the last 12 months, were you looking for work?	
Q3: What is the main reason you did NOT look for work on the last 12 months? (SKIP if Q2 = NO) 01 = Stay at home parent/childcare 02 = Student 03 = Disabled/illness 04 = No jobs available 05 = Tried and did not succeed in the past 06 = Was treated badly at work	
Q4: If you are working, do any of the statements below apply to your work experience? (Check all that apply) 01 = Low pay/low income 02 = Hard work/too tiresome 03 = Long or unpredictable hours 04 = Distance/time it takes to the workplace 05 = Treated badly/discriminated at work 06 = No benefits (health insurance, annual leave, etc.)	
Q5: Over the past five years, have you had any work-related training that lasted at least 4 days (could be non-consecutive) and that is/was not part of your formal education? 01 = Yes 02 = No	

TIME-USE

These questions are about how you spend your time. For each question, please record the number of hours.

Q1: How many hours you sleep on a typical night?	
Q2: How many hours per week do you spend caring for others (younger children, ill household members, etc.)?	
Q3: How many hours per week do you spend on domestic tasks (cleaning, cooking, shopping, household repairs)?	
Q4: How many hours per week to you spend on activities to earn money (outside the house)?	
Q5: How many hours per week do you spend on community service or other forms of volunteering?	

Q6: How many hours per week do you spend at college or other school, including travel time?	
Q7: How many hours per week do you spend using the internet, including playing video games?	
Q8: How many hours per week do you spend seeing friends?	
Q9: How many hours per week do you spend on outdoor activities— sports, biking, walking?	

Section 5: Migration

These questions are about whether you have ever thought of moving to somewhere else. For each question, unless otherwise stated, 01 = YES; 02 = NO; 03 = OTHER

Q1: In the next 10 years, would you like to move to another town, county, or city (inside or outside the country)?	
Q2: If you were to move, where would you most likely move to? 01 = Different neighborhood within the same county 02 = Different county, same state 03 = Different state, same region 04 = Different state, on the coasts 05 = Different country 06 = Other (specify):	
Q3: What are the main reasons why you would move if you had the opportunity to? (Check all that apply) 01 = For better jobs, opportunities 02 = To continue my education 03 = For better public services or connectivity 04 = For less crime and violence 05 = Significant other or related family reasons 06 = Other	
Q4: What are the main reasons why you would NOT move? Please record up to three reasons in order of importance. 01 = I am studying here 02 = My community/home is here 03 = My family is here 04 = I am happy here 05 = I do not have the skills of finances to move	

Section 6: Feelings and Aspirations

FEELINGS, ATTITUDES, AND PERCEPTIONS

This section asks your opinion about different things. There are no right or wrong answers. There are four options: 01 = Strongly disagree ; 02 = Disagree; 03 = Agree; 05 = Strongly; and 00 = Not Know

	01 = Strongly disagree	02 = Disagree	03 = Agree	04 = Strongly agree	00 = Not Know
Q1: I make friends easily.					
Q2: I know that my life will be better in the future.					

Q3: The important people in my life tell me that I will have a successful life.					
Q4: I trust that I will achieve the goals that I set for myself.					
Q5: I get along well with my parents.					
Q6: I can always manage to solve difficult problems if I try hard enough.					

ASPIRATIONS

Now we are going to ask you about your aspirations about your education.

Q1: What level of education would you like to achieve? 01 = High school degree or GED 02 = Certificate or technical degree 03 = Associate's degree 04 = Bachelor's degree 05 = Graduate or professional school	
Q2: Given your current situation do you expect you will reach that level of education? 01 = Yes 02 = No 03 = Don't Know	
Q3: What is the main obstacle to achieving this? 01 = Lack of education/skills 02 = Economic constraints 03 = Lack of parental support 04 = Lack of social networks 05 = Frequent illness 06 = Uncertainty due to the COVID-19 pandemic	

HOPE

These questions are about your future and your hope for success. Please tell me how much you agree with the following statements about yourself on a scale of one to four: 01 = Strongly disagree; 02 = Disagree; 03 = Agree; 04 = Strongly agree; 00 = Not Know

	01 = Strongly disagree	02 = Disagree	03 = Agree	04 = Strongly agree	00 = Not Know
Q1: I trust that I will be able to do everything that I want to do in my future.					
Q2: I believe that the things I am doing now are preparing me for what I want in the future.					

Q3: I believe that I will be successful even when there are difficulties in my life now.					
Q4: There are people who can help me when I need guidance to achieve something important to me.					
Q5: Are you still hopeful about your future since the onset of the COVID-19 pandemic?					

Section 7: Subjective Wealth

Think about this town.	
Q1: Compared to other households here in your neighborhood, would you describe your household at the moment as: 01 = High income 02 = About average 03 = A little less income than most households 04 = Among the lowest income	
Now think about the household where you live.	
Q2: Which of the following best describes your household's financial situation? 01 = Wealthy 02 = Comfortable—can manage to get by 03 = Never have quite enough, struggle to get by 04 = Poor	
Now think about the unexpected.	
Q3: How confident are you that you could come up with $2,000 if a financial emergency arose within the next month? 01 = I am certain I could come up with the full $2,000 02 = I could probably come up with $2,000 03 = I could probably not come up with $2,000 04 = I could not come up with $2,000	

Section 8: Marital and Living Arrangement

BASIC INFORMATION AND MATCHING

Q1: What is your current marital status? 01 = Cohabitant 02 = Separated 03 = Married 04 = Widow/widower 05 = Divorced 06 = Single	
Please answer the following questions if you are or have ever been married or cohabited with someone.	

Q1: Is your current or most recent spouse/partner currently living in the same household? 01 = Yes, lives in household 02 = No, lives elsewhere temporarily 03 = No, lives elsewhere permanently	
Q2: Do you have a child/children? If yes, how many?	
Q3: Do they live with you? 01 = Yes 02 = No	
Q4: How many people (total) live in the house?	
Q5: How many are children?	

Section 9: Health

HEALTH

These questions are about your physical health.

Q1: In general, would you say your health is very poor, poor, average, good or very good? 01 = Very poor 02 = Poor 03 = Average 04 = Good 05 = Very good	
Q2: Compared with other men/women of your same age would you say your health is, the same, much better, better, worse or much worse? 01 = Much worse 02 = Worse 03 = Same 04 = Better 05 = Much better	

SERIOUS INJURIES AND ILLNESS

Q1: Over the past five years, have you been seriously injured? How many times did this happen? (A serious injury is one that prevents you from doing normal activities [school, work, etc.] and/or that requires medical attention.) 01 = 1 time 02 = More than 1 time	
Q2: Over the past five years, have you been seriously ill? (Serious illnesses are illnesses which prevent you from doing normal activities [school, work, etc.] and/or require medical attention. For example, asthma, gastritis, anemia, epilepsy, etc.) 01 = Yes 02 = No	

Section 10: Public Programs

These about some key services you may have access to. For each question, unless otherwise stated, 01 = YES; 02 = NO; 03 = OTHER

Q1: Do you have a Social Security Card?	
Q2: Do you have health insurance?	
Q3: If yes, which type of health insurance (private, from employer, ACA, Medicaid, etc.)?	
Q4: Below is a list of several government benefit programs. In the past 6 months, have you or someone in your household participated in each of the following programs? For each question, 01 = YES; 02 = NO	
Food Stamps (SNAP)	
Temporary Assistance for Needy Families (TANF)	
Public housing/Housing Choice Voucher	
Women, Infants, and Children (WIC)	
Head Start	
LIHEAP/utility assistance from government	
Unemployment Benefits	
Pell Grants (Pell Grants are funding from the government to help students pay for college)	
Social Security (supplemental, survivor, retirement, disability, etc.)	
Q5: In the past 6 months, how many times did you or someone in your household receive assistance from a nonprofit or religious organization to help you meet your basic needs (for example, food, clothing, shelter, money, or medical care)? 01 = Never 02 = Once 03 = 2–3 times 04 = 4 or more times 05 = I don't know	
Q6: In the past 6 months, how many times did you or someone in your tax household receive Earned Income Tax Credit (EITC)? EITC is a tax benefit for working people with low to moderate income. 01 = Never 02 = Once 03 = 2–3 times 04 = 4 or more times 05 = I don't know	

Section 11: Social Capital

SYSTEM/SUPPORT NETWORK

For each question, 01 = YES; 02 = NO; 03 = OTHER

Q1: Suppose you are in need of material support, such as money, lodging, or transportation. Do you have friends of family you can rely on in times of need?	
Q2: Do you have close relatives living in this neighborhood? (exclude those from your own home)?	

Q3: Generally, do you feel that people in your neighborhood can be trusted? 01 = All of the time 02 = Some of the time 03 = Not at all	
Q4: Generally, do you feel safe walking alone in your neighborhood? 01 = All of the time 02 = Some of the time 03 = Not at all	

FAMILY SUPPORT

Q1: Which adult was most involved in your schooling until now? 01 = Mother 02 = Father 03 = Older sibling 04 = Aunt or Uncle 05 = Grandparent 06 = Other, please specify 07 = No Adult	
Q2: How much schooling does she/he hope you will attain? 01 = Finish the current year and no more 02 = Attain university 03 = Attain master or doctoral program	

Section 12: Economic Changes

The following are questions about your current circumstances and how and why they might have changed over the past 2 years. For each question, unless otherwise stated, 01 = YES; 02 = NO; 03 = OTHER

Q1: In the last years, has the household been the victim of any crime? For example, theft, robbery, or burglary.	
Q2: Have there been any changes within the family over the past years? Or other things that have affected members of the family? For each question, 01 = YES; 02 = NO	
Death of a parent	
Illness of a parent or other household member	
Divorce, separation or abandonment	
Birth/new household member	
Child's school enrollment—having to pay fees	
Q3: Have any of the events listed above led you to have to take out a loan, skip a housing, medical or child care payment?	
Q4: In the last 6 months, have you or has anyone in your household: For each question, 01 = YES; 02 = NO	
Lost a job unexpectedly (including due to the COVID-19 pandemic)	
Had an unexpected reduction in income (including due to the COVID-19 pandemic)	
Did your household fall behind on payments or go into collections for your credit card(s) as a result of the COVID-19 pandemic?	

Had an unexpected major house, appliance or vehicle repair	
Had unexpected legal expenses	
Had unexpected major medical expense (e.g., from hospitalization or emergency room visit)	

Section 13: Preferences

TIME DISCOUNTING

The following are a series of hypothetical statements. They are imaginary, but we would like you to answer as you would if this really happened to you. For each question, select option A or option B.

Q1: Imagine you just won the lottery or had other such luck, but you have two options to receive your money. Would you prefer to receive: Option A: $500 immediately guaranteed Option B: $600 in 1 month guaranteed	
Q2: Now imagine you just won the lottery or had other such luck, but you have two options to receive your money. Would you prefer to receive: Option A: $500 immediately guaranteed Option B: $800 in 1 month guaranteed	

RISK-TAKING

The following is a series of statements. Please indicate whether you strongly agree, agree, disagree, or strongly disagree with the statement.

	01 = Strongly disagree	02 = Disagree	03 = Agree	04 = Strongly agree	00 = Not Know
Q1: Relative to other people, I am willing to take risks in my life.					
Q2: If I get money, I tend to spend it too quickly.					
Q3: I tend to avoid thinking about the future.					

SAVINGS AND CREDIT

These questions are about your savings and credit decisions. For each question, unless otherwise stated, 01 = YES; 02 = NO; 03 = OTHER

Q1: How much do you currently have saved in bank accounts, at home, or elsewhere?	
Q2: People decide to save or not save money for a variety of reasons, including future predictions about their income. Do you think about the future when you make your decisions about spending and saving? 01 = YES 02 = NO, I do not have enough money 03 = NO, I do not think about the future	
Q3: Do you have any debts that impact your savings? These include on credit cards, student loans, loans from friends/family?	

LOCUS OF CONTROL

For each of the following questions, please indicate whether you: Strongly disagree = 01; Disagree = 02; Agree = 03; or Strongly agree = 04

	01 = Strongly disagree	02 = Disagree	03 = Agree	04 = Strongly agree	00 = Not Know
Q1: When I get what I want, it is usually because I worked hard for it.					
Q2: My life is determined by my own actions.					
Q3: I feel like what happens in my life is mostly determined by powerful people, like parents, friends, or external forces.					

Section 14: Feelings, Behaviors, and Emotions

FEELINGS

The first questions are about how you get along with your parents/guardians and how you feel about things at home. For each statement choose whether this statement is "completely true for you," "a little true for you" or "not true for you."

Statements	Completely true for you	A little true for you	Not true for you
1. You usually feel able to speak about your views and feelings with your parents/guardians.	☐	☐	☐
2. Most of the time your parents/guardians treat you fairly when you do something wrong.	☐	☐	☐

SMOKING

The next few questions are about smoking cigarettes or vaping.

3. How many of your best friends smoke cigarettes or vape at least once a week? Choose only one option.
☐ Most of my friends
☐ few of my friends
☐ None of my friends

4. How many of the following people smoke? You can choose more than one option.
☐ Parents/guardians
☐ Brothers/sisters
☐ Boyfriend/girlfriend
☐ Your best friend
☐ None of the above
5. How old were you when you tried a cigarette for the first time? Choose only one option.
☐ 13 years old or younger
☐ 14 years old–18 years old ☐ I have never smoked or vaped

FRIENDS AND VIOLENCE

We know that in many communities young people like yourself are hurt or treated badly by other people. The next few questions ask about things that have happened to you and your friends.

6. Have you ever been beaten up or physically hurt in other ways by the following people? You can choose more than one option.
☐ Somebody from your family
☐ Boyfriend/girlfriend/spouse
☐ Stranger
☐ Friend
☐ Teacher
☐ Boss
☐ I have never been beaten up or hurt
7. During the last 30 days, on how many days did you carry a weapon such as a knife or gun to be able to protect yourself? Choose only one option.
☐ 1 day
☐ 2 to 3 days
☐ More than 4 days
☐ Never
8. How many of your best friends have been or are members of a gang? Choose only one option.
☐ Most of my friends
☐ A few of my friends
☐ None of my friends
9. Have you ever been a member of a gang? Choose only one option.
☐ Yes
☐ No
10. Have you ever been arrested by the police or have you been arrested for any crime? Choose only one option.
☐ Yes
☐ No

11. Have you ever been sentenced to spend time in a correctional facility such as a jail or prison, or in a juvenile detention center, or have you had to do community service? Choose only one option.
☐ Yes
☐ No

ALCOHOL

The next questions ask you about your experiences with alcohol.

12. How many of your best friends drink alcohol at least once a month? Choose only one option.
☐ Most of my friends
☐ A few of my friends
☐ None of my friends
13. How often do you usually drink alcohol? Choose only one option.
☐ Every day
☐ At least once a week
☐ At least once a month
☐ Never
14. Have you ever been drunk from too much alcohol? Choose only one option.
☐ I never drink alcohol
☐ Yes
☐ No

15. During your life, have you ever tried one of the following drugs? IF yes, please choose with (X) and say how old were you when you first tried it.

	Yes, very often	Yes, sometimes	Just once	No, never	How old were you when you tried it for the first time?
Inhalants	☐	☐	☐	☐	_ _ years
Marijuana	☐	☐	☐	☐	_ _ years
Opioids	☐	☐	☐	☐	_ _ years
Other drugs (crack, heroine, fentanyl, etc.)	☐	☐	☐	☐	_ _ years

SEX

Many young people your age think a lot about sex. Many already have had sex. The following questions are about sex and what you know about it. For each of the statements below, decide:

16. Where would you go to get information on sexual matters? Choose only one option.

☐ Planned Parenthood or health center

☐ Pharmacy

☐ The decision is left to my girlfriend/boyfriend/spouse

☐ I don't need information on sexual matters

☐ I don't know

	True	False	I don't know
17. A woman/ girl cannot get pregnant the first time she has sex.	☐	☐	☐
18. A person can get HIV the first time he/she has sex.	☐	☐	☐

19. How old were you when you had sex for the first time? Choose only one option.

☐ 13–14 years old, or less

☐ 15–16 years old

☐ 17–18 years old

☐ older than 18 years old

☐ I never had sex

20. The last time you had sex, what did you do to prevent getting pregnant or a disease? You can choose more than one option.

☐ I never had sex

☐ We used a condom

☐ Use after morning pill

☐ Use other birth control

☐ We did not use any method

☐ I don't know if we use any method

21. Have you ever had sex when you did not want to? Choose only one option.

☐ Yes, one time

☐ Yes, more than once

☐ No

SADNESS

This part of the questionnaire looks at sadness and other difficulties that many people experience at some point in their lives. As you answer, think about how things have been for you in the last 6 months. It would be great if you could try to answer all the questions even if you are not sure of the answer or if the question seems stupid.

Answers	Completely true for you	A little true for you	Not true for you
22. You worry a lot.	☐	☐	☐

23. You get a lot of headaches, stomachaches or sickness.	☐	☐	☐
24. You are often unhappy, downhearted or tearful.	☐	☐	☐
25. You worry more since the onset of COVID-19.	☐	☐	☐

HAPPINESS

The last part of the questionnaire looks at what makes you happy.

26. What makes you happy? You can choose more than one option.
☐ Spending time with my friends
☐ Spending time with my family
☐ Doing some exercise (playing soccer, dancing, etc.)
☐ Other, specify: _____

THANK YOU FOR YOUR PARTICIPATION.

Section for Interviewers

TO START: BASIC INFORMATION

Location of interview	
Date/time of interview	
Interviewer Information	

Interviewer: I declare that I have complied with the Assent / Consent process informing of the Youth in the previous text.	
Name: _____	Signature: _____
ID: _____	Date: __ __ / __ __ / ____ (day) (month) (year)
	End time: __ __ : __ __

Date: __ __ / __ __ / ____	Start time: __ __ : __ __
Age: _____	Gender: ☐ Female ☐ Male

REFERENCES

Abler, Laurie et al. 2017. "Hope Matters: Developing and Validating a Measure of Future Expectations among Young Women in a High HIV Prevalence Setting in Rural South Africa (HPTN 068)." *AIDS and Behavior* 21 (7): 2156.

Aizer, A., Eli, S., Ferrie, J., and Lleras-Muney, A. 2016. "The Long-Run Impact of Cash Transfers to Poor Families." *American Economic Review* 106 (4): 935–71.

Almlund, M., Duckworth, A. L., Heckman, J., and Kautz, T. 2011. "Personality Psychology and Economics." In *Handbook of the Economics of Education*. Vol. 4, 2011, North Holland.

Alos-Ferrer, C. 2018. "A Review Essay on Social Neuroscience: Can Research on the Social Brain and Economics Inform Each Other?" *Journal of Economic Literature* 56 (1): 234–64.

Amabile, T. and Pratt, M. 2016. "The Dynamic Componential Model of Creativity and Innovation in Organizations: Making Progress, Making Meaning." *Research in Organizational Behavior* 36: 157–83.

Andrade-Chaico, F. and Andrade-Arenas, L. 2019. "Projections on Insecurity, Unemployment and Poverty and Their Consequences in Lima's District San Juan de Lurigancho in the Next 10 years." *IEEE Sciences and Humanities International Research Conference*: 1–4. https://doi.org/10.1109/SHIRCON48091.2019.9024877.

Appadurai, A. 2004. "The Capacity to Aspire: Culture and the Terms of Recognition." In *Culture and Public Action*, edited by V. Rao and M. Walton, 59–84. Stanford: Stanford University Press.

Ashraf, Q. and Galor, O. 2013. "The Out of Africa Hypothesis, Human Genetic Diversity and Comparative Economic Development." *American Economic Review* 102: 1–46.

Assari, S. 2017. "General Self-Efficacy and Mortality: Racial and Ethnic Differences in the U.S.A." *Journal of Racial-Ethnic Health Disparities* 4 (4).

Assari, S., Gibbons, F., and Simons, R. 2018. "Depression among Black Youth: The Intersection of Race and Place." *Brain Sciences* 108 (8).

Atkinson, R., Muro, M., and Whiton, J. 2019. "The Case for Growth Centers: How to Spread Tech Innovation across America," Brookings Institution Report, Washington, D.C. December.

Baird, S., de Hoop, J., and Özler, B. 2013. "Income Shocks and Adolescent Mental Health." *Journal of Human Resources* 48 (2): 370–403.

Bandura, A., Barbaranelli, C., Caprara, G. V., and Pastorelli, C. 2001. "Self-Efficacy Beliefs as Shapers of Children's Aspirations and Career Trajectories." *Child Development* 72 (1): 187–206. https://doi.org/10.1111/1467-8624.00273.

Beal, S. J. and Crockett, L. J. 2010. "Adolescents' Occupational and Educational Aspirations and Expectations: Links to High School Activities and Adult Educational Attainment." *Developmental Psychology* 46 (1): 258–65. https://doi.org/10.1037/a0017416.

Beaman, L., Duflo, E., Pande, R., and Topalova, P. 2012. "Female Leadership Raises Aspirations and Educational Attainment for Girls: A Policy Experiment in India." *Science* 335 (6068): 582–86. https://doi.org/10.1126/science.1212382

Benjamin, D. J., Cesarini, D., Chabris, C. F., Glaeser, E. L., Laibson, D. I., Gunason, V., and Lichtenstein, P. 2012. "The Promises and Pitfalls of Genoeconomics." *Annual Review of Economics* 4.

Bernard, T., Dercon, S., Orkin, K., and Taffesse, A. 2014. "The Future in Mind: Aspirations and Forwardlooking Behaviour in Rural Ethiopia." *CSAE Working Paper Series.* 2014–16.

Bernard, T. and Taffesse, A. 2014. "Aspirations: An Approach to Measurement with Validation Using Ethiopian Data." *Journal of African Economies* 23 (2): 189–224. https://doi.org/10.1093/jae/ejt030.

———. 2012. "Measuring Aspirations: Discussion and Example from Ethiopia," International Food Policy Research Institute Discussion Paper.

Blakemore, S. J. and Mills, K. L. 2014. "Is Adolescence a Sensitive Period for Sociocultural Processing?" *Annual Review of Psychology* 65 (1): 187–207.

Blanchflower, D. and Bryson, A. 2021. "Biden, COVID and Mental Health in America." Working Paper 29040. National Bureau of Economic Research. http://www.nber.org/papers/w29040.

Blanchflower, D. and Graham, C. 2021. "The Mid-Life Dip in Well-Being: A Critique." *Social Indicators Research* 161 (August): 287–344.

Blanchflower, D. and Oswald, A. 2019. "Unhappiness and Pain in America: A Review Essay, and Further Evidence, on Carol Graham's *Happiness for All?*" *Journal of Economic Literature* 57 (2): 385–402.

Blum, R. and Boyden, J. 2018. "Understand the Lives of Youth in Low-Income Countries." *Nature* 554 (7693): 435–37. https://www.nature.com/articles/d41586-018-02107-w.

Bonney, S. and Stickley, T. 2008. "Recovery and Mental Health: A Review of the British Literature." *Journal of Psychiatric and Mental Health Nursing* 15 (2): 140–53.

Borghans, L., Duckworth, A., Heckman, J., and Ter Weel, B. 2008. "The Economics and Psychology of Personality Traits." *Journal of Human Resources* 43 (4).

Brickman, P. and Campbell, D. 1971. "Hedonic Relativism and Planning the Good Society." In *Adaptation Theory: A Symposium*, edited by M. Apley. New York: Academic Press.

Brooks, A. 2021. "The Difference Between Hope and Optimism." *The Atlantic,* September.

Burtless, G. 2009. "Demographic Transformation and Economic Inequality." In *The Oxford Handbook of Economic Inequality*, edited by W. Salverda, B. Nolan, and T. Smeeding, 435–54. Oxford: Oxford University Press.

Case, A. and Deaton, A. 2015. "Rising Morbidity and Mortality in Midlife among White Non-Hispanic Americans in the 21st Century." *Proceedings of the National Academy of Sciences* 112 (49): 15078–15083.

Case, A., Deaton, A., and Stone, A. 2020. "Decoding the Mystery of American Pain Reveals Warning for the Future." *Proceedings of the National Academy of Sciences* 117 (40): 24785–24789.

Caspi, A. et al. 2003. "Influence of Life Stress on Depression: Moderation by a Polymorphism in the 5-HTT Gene." *Science* 301.

Cherlin, A. 2019. "In the Shadow of Sparrows Point: Racialized Labor in the White and Black Working Classes." Russell Sage Working Paper, New York, October.

Clark, A. E. 2019. "Born to Be Mild? Cohort Effects Don't (Fully) Explain Why Well-Being Is U-Shaped in Age." In *The Economics of Happiness: How the Easterlin Paradox Transformed Our Understanding of Well-Being and Progress*, edited by M. Rojas, 387–408. Cham, Switzerland: Springer.

Clark, C., Fleche, S., Layard, R., Powdthavee, N., and Ward, G. 2018. *The Origins of Happiness: The Science of Well-Being over the Life Course*. Princeton, NJ: Princeton University Press.

Clark, D. 2018. "Realizing the Mass Public Benefits of Evidence-Based Psychological Therapies: The IAPT Program." *Annual Review of Clinical Psychology* 14: 159–83.

Copeland, W., Gaydosh, Hill, S., Godwin, J., Mullan Harris, S., Costello, J., and Shanahan, L. 2020. "Associations of Despair with Suicidality and Substance Misuse Among Young Adults." *JAMA Network Open* 3 (6).

Cotofan, M., DeNeve, J. E., Goin, M., Katz, M., and Ward, G. 2021. "Work and Well-Being during COVID-19: Impact, Inequalities, Resilience, and the Future of Work." *World Happiness Report 2021*. Sustainable Development Network.

Dalton, P. S., Ghosal, S., and Mani, A. 2016. "Poverty and Aspirations Failure." *Economic Journal* 126 (590): 165–88. https://doi.org/10.1111/ecoj.12210.

DaSilva, J. 2021. *We're Still Here: Pain and Politics in the Heart of America*. Oxford: Oxford University Press.

Dasey, J. 2018. "The U.K. Now Has a Minister of Loneliness: Here's Why It Matters." *Smithsonian Magazine*, January 19.

Davis, L. and Wu, S. 2014. "Social Comparisons and Life Satisfaction across Racial and Ethnic Groups: The Effects of Status, Information, and Solidarity." *Social Indicators Research* 117: 849–69.

Deci, E. M. and Ryan, R. M. 1985. *Intrinsic Motivation and Human Behavior*. New York: Plenum.

De Neve, J. E., Christakis, N., Fowler, J., and Frey, B. 2012. "Genes, Economics, and Happiness." *Journal of Neuroscience, Psychology, and Economics* 5 (4): 193–211.

De Neve, J. E., and Oswald, A. E. 2012. "Estimating the Influence of Life Satisfaction and Positive Affect on Later Income Using Sibling Fixed Effects." *Proceedings of the National Academy of Sciences* 109 (49).

Dercon, S. and Singh, A. 2013. "From Nutrition to Aspirations and Self-Efficacy: Gender Bias over Time among Children in Four Countries." *World Development* 45 (71). https://doi.org/10.1016/j.worlddev.2012.12.001.

Diener, E., Suh, E. M., Lucas, R. E. and Smith, H. L. 1999. "Subjective Well-Being: Three Decades of Progress." *Psychological Bulletin* 125: 276–302.

Dieter, W., Copeland, W., Angold, A., and Costello J. E. 2013. "Impact of Bullying in Childhood on Adult Health, Wealth, Crime, and Social Outcomes." *Psychology Science* 24 (10): 1958–70.

Dobson, E., Graham, C., and Dodd, E. 2021. "When Public Health Crises Become Entwined: How Trends in COVID-19, Deaths of Despair, and Well-Being Track across the U.S.A." *Annals of the American Academy of Political and Social Science* 698.

Dobson, E., Graham, C., Hua, T., and Pinto S. 2022. "Despair and Resilience in the U.S.: Did the COVID Pandemic Worsen Mental Health Outcomes?" Brookings Institution Report, April 2022. https://www.brookings.edu/research/despair

-and-resilience-in-the-us-did-the-covid-pandemic-worsen-mental-health
-outcomes/.

Easterlin, A. R., McVey, M., Switek, M., Sarafanga, O., and Smith-Ryan, J. 2010. "The Happiness-Income Paradox Re-Visited." *Proceedings of the National Academy of Sciences* 107 (52): 22463–22468.

Edsall, T. 2021a. "White Riot." *New York Times,* January 13.

———. 2021b. "How the Storming of the Capitol Became a 'Normal Tourist Visit,'" *New York Times,* May 19.

Eyre, Harris et al. 2021. "Build Brains Better: A Proposal for a White House Brain Capital Council to Accelerate Post-Covid Recovery and Resilience." *Brookings Institution Report.* Washington, D.C. (December).

Feuer, A. 2021. "Fears of White People Losing Out Permeate Capitol Rioters' Towns, Study Finds." *New York Times,* April 6.

Figlio, D., Giuliano, P., Özek, U., and Sapienza, P. 2019. "Long-Term Orientation and Educational Performance." *American Economic Journal: Economic Policy* 11 (4): 272–309.

Ford, T. 2022. "Trying to Make a Change: How Black Middle-Class Women Support Their Own Wellbeing in the United States." *Ethnicity and Health* (forthcoming).

Forget, E. L. 2011. "The Town with No Poverty: The Health Effects of a Canadian Guaranteed Annual Income Field Experiment." *Canadian Public Policy* 37 (3): 283–305.

Frederick, S. W. and Loewenstein, G. 1999. "Hedonic Adaptation." In *Well-Being: The Foundations of Hedonic Psychology*, edited by D. Kahneman, E. Diener, and N. Schwarz, 302–29. New York: Russell Sage Foundation.

Frey, B. and Stutzer, A. 2002. "What Can Economists Learn from Happiness Research?" *Journal of Economic Literature* 40 (2): 402–35.

Fruttero, A., Muller, N., and Calvo-Gonzalez, O. "The Power and Roots of Aspirations: A Survey of the Empirical Evidence." Policy Research Working Paper Series 9729, The World Bank.

Gallagher, M., Long, L., and Phillips, C. 2020. "Hope, Optimism, Self-Efficacy, and Posttraumatic Stress Disorder: A Meta-Analytic Review of the Protective Effects of Positive Expectancies." *Journal of Clinical Psychology* 76 (3): 329–355.

Galor, O., and Özak, Ö. 2016. "The Agricultural Origins of Time Preference." *American Economic Review* 106 (10): 3064–3103.

Genicot, G. and Ray, D. 2017. "Aspirations and Inequality." *Econometrica* 85 (2): 489–519. https://doi.org/10.3982/ecta13865.

Goodman, R. 1997. "The Strengths and Difficulties Questionnaire: A Research Note." *Journal of Child Psychology and Psychiatry* 38 (5): 581–86.

Gottfredson, L. S. 2002. "Gottfredson's Theory of Circumscription, Compromise, and Self-Creation." In *Career Choice and Development*, edited by D. Brown, 85–148. San Francisco: Jossey-Bass.

Gottfredson, L. S. 2002a. "g: Highly General and Highly Practical." In *The General Factor of Intelligence: How General Is It?* Edited by R. J. Sternberg and E. L. Grigorenko, 331–380. Mahwah, NJ: Erlbaum.

Gould, E. 2021. "Torn Apart? The Impact of Manufacturing Employment Decline on Black and White Americans." *Review of Economics and Statistics* 103 (4): 770–85.

Graham, C. 2011. "Adaptation amidst Prosperity and Adversity: Insights from Happiness Studies from around the World." *World Bank Research Observer* 26 (1): 105–37. https://doi.org/10.1093/wbro/lkq004.

———. 2009. *Happiness around the World: The Paradox of Happy Peasants and Miserable Millionaires.* Oxford: Oxford University Press.

———. 2017. *Happiness for All? Unequal Hopes and Lives in Pursuit of the American Dream.* Princeton, NJ: Princeton University Press.

———. 2020. "The Human Costs of the Pandemic: Is It Time to Prioritize Well-Being?" Brookings Institution. https://www.brookings.edu/research/the-human-costs -of-the-pandemic-is-it-time-to-prioritize-well-being/.

Graham, C., Chung, Y., Grinstein-Weiss, M., and Roll, S. 2022. "Well-Being and Mental Health amid COVID-19: Differences in Resilience across Minorities and Whites." *PLOS One,* forthcoming.

Graham, C., Eggers, A., and Sukhtankar, S. 2004. "Does Happiness Pay? An Exploration Based on Panel Data from Russia." *Journal of Economic Behavior and Organization* 55 (3): 319–42. https://doi.org/10.1016/j.jebo.2003.09.002.

Graham, C., and MacLennan, S. 2020. "Policy Insights from the New Science of Well-Being." *Behavioral Science and Policy* 6 (1).

Graham, C. and Nikolova, M. 2015. "In Transit: The Well-Being of Migrants from Transition and Post-Transition Countries." *Journal of Economic Behavior & Organization* 112 (C): 164–86.

Graham, C. and Pettinato, S. 2002. *Happiness and Hardship: Opportunity and Insecurity in New Market Economies.* Washington DC: The Brookings Institution Press.

Graham, C. and Pinto, S. 2019. "Unequal Hopes and Lives in the USA: Optimism, Race, Place, and Premature Mortality." *Journal of Population Economics* 32: 665–733.

———. 2021. "The Geography of Desperation in America: Labor Force Participation, Mobility, Place, and Well-Being." *Social Science and Medicine* 270 (113612).

Graham, C. and Ruiz-Pozuelo, J. 2022. "Do High Aspirations Lead to Better Outcomes? Evidence from a Longitudinal Survey of Adolescents in Peru." *Journal of Population Economics.*

Gustavson, K., von Soest, T., Karevold, E., and Røysamb, E. 2012. "Attrition and Generalizability in Longitudinal Studies: Findings from a 15-Year Population-Based Study and a Monte Carlo Simulation Study." *BMC Public Health* 12 (1): 1–11. https://doi.org/10.1186/1471-2458-12-918.

Hall, C., Zhao, J., and Shafir, E. 2013. "Self-Affirmation among the Poor: Cognitive and Behavioral Implications." *Psychological Science* 25 (2): 619–25.

Haushofer, J. and Fehr, E. 2014. "On the Psychology of Poverty." *Science* 344 (6186): 862–67.

Hayes, S. C. 2007. *ACT in Action DVD series.* Oakland, CA: New Harbinger.

Heckman, J. and Kautz, T. 2012. "Hard Evidence on Soft Skills." *Labour Economics* 19 (4): 451–64. https://doi.org/10.1016/j.labeco.2012.05.014.

Helliwell, J., Huang, H., and Wang, S. 2018. "New Evidence on Trust and Well-Being." In *Oxford Handbook of Social and Political Trust,* edited by Eric M. Uslaner, 409. Oxford: Oxford Handbooks.

Herrin, J., Witters, D., Roy, B., Riley, C., Liu, D., and Krumholz, H. M. 2018. "Population Well-Being and Electoral Shifts." *PLOS One* 13 (3).

Hill, F. 2021. *There is Nothing for You Here: Finding Opportunity in the 21st Century*. New York: HarperCollins.

Hofstede, G. 2001. *Culture's Consequences: Comparing Values, Behaviors, Institutions, and Organizations across Nations*. London: Sage Publications.

Hothshild, A. 2016. *Strangers in Their Own Land*. New York: New Press.

Hoxby, C. 2021. "Advanced Cognitive Skill Deserts in the U.S.: Their Likely Causes and Implications." *Brookings Papers on Economic Activity*. March.

Hufe, P., Kanbur, R., and Peichle, A. "Measuring Unfair Inequality: Reconciling Equality of Opportunity and Freedom from Poverty." *Review of Economic Studies* 1: 1–36.

International Labour Office. *International Standard Classification of Occupations: ISCO-08*. Geneva.

Isenberg, N. 2017. *White Trash: The 400 Year-Untold Story of Class in America*. New York: Penguin-Random House Books.

Jensen, R. 2010. "The (Perceived) Returns to Education and the Demand for Schooling." *Quarterly Journal of Economics* 125 (2): 515–48.

Joe, S., Baser, R., Neighbors, H., Caldwell, C., and Jackson, J. 2009. "12-Month and Lifetime Prevalence of Suicide Attempts among Black Adolescents in the National Survey of American Life." *Journal of the American Academy of Child and Adolescent Psychiatry* 48 (3): 271–82.

Kahneman D. and Deaton A. 2010. "High Income Improves Evaluation of Life but Not Emotional Well-Being." *Proceedings of the National Academy of Sciences of the United States of America* 107 (38): 16489–16493.

Kanazawa, S. and Lopez, T. 2021. "Why Amish Babies Don't Cry and the Danes Are the Happiest People: The Selective Outmigration by Personality Type Hypothesis." Working Paper, *London School of Economics*.

Kaufman, J. and Sternberg, R., eds. 2019. *The Cambridge Handbook of Creativity*, 2nd ed., Cambridge Handbooks in Psychology. Cambridge: Cambridge University Press.

Kaufman, S. B. 2021. "The Opposite of Toxic Positivity." *The Atlantic*, August.

Kerpelman, J. L., Eryigit, S., and Stephens, C. J. 2008. "African American Adolescents' Future Education Orientation: Associations with Self-Efficacy, Ethnic Identity, and Perceived Parental Support." *Journal of Youth and Adolescence* 37 (8): 997–1008. https://doi.org/10.1007/s10964-007-9201-7.

Kessler, R. C., Berglund, P., Demler, O., Jin, R., Merikangas, K. R., and Walters, E. E. 2005. "Lifetime Prevalence and Age-of-Onset Distributions of DSM-IV Disorders in the National Comorbidity Survey Replication." *Archives of General Psychiatry* 62 (6): 593–602.

Kokuban, K., Nemoto, N., and Yamakawa, Y. 2022. "Brain Conditions Mediate the Association Between Age and Happiness." *Scientific Reports*, forthcoming.

Krekel, C., De Neve, J. E., Fancourt, D., and Layard, R. 2021. "A Local Community Course That Raises Wellbeing and Pro-Sociality: Evidence from a Randomized Controlled Trial." *Journal of Economic Behavior and Organization* 188: 322–36.

Kubzansky L. D., Winning A., and Kawachi, I. 2014. "Affective States and Health." In *Social Epidemiology: New Perspectives on Social Determinants of Global Population Health*, edited by L. F. Berkman, M. M. Glymour, and I. Kawachi, 2nd edition. New York: Oxford University Press.

La Ferrara, E., Chong, A., and Duryea, S. 2012. "Soap Operas and Fertility: Evidence from Brazil." *American Economic Journal: Applied Economics* 4 (4): 1–31. https://doi.org/10.1257/app.4.4.1.

Layard, R. 2005. *Happiness: Lessons from a New Science*. London: Penguin Books.

Lerner, M. 1982. *The Belief in a Just World: A Fundamental Disillusion*. New York: Plenum Press.

Levelling Up the United Kingdom. London: U.K. Government, Department of Levelling Up, Housing, and Communities. https://www.gov.uk/government/publications/levelling-up-the-united-kingdom.

Levenson, H. 1974. "Activism and Powerful Others: Distinctions within the Concept of Internal-External Control." *Journal of Personality Assessment* 38 (4): 377–83. https://doi.org/10.1080/00223891.1974.10119988.

Liberini, F., Redoano, M., and Proto, E. 2017. "Happy Voters." *Journal of Public Economics* 146 (C): 41–57.

Lister, C., O'Keefe, M., Salunkhe, S., and Edmonds, T. 2021. "Cultural Well-Being Index: A Dynamic Cultural Analytics Process for Measuring and Managing Organizational Inclusion as an Antecedent Condition of Employee Well-Being and Innovation Capacity." *Journal of Organizational Psychology*, forthcoming.

Lordon, G. and McGuire, A. 2019. "Widening the High School Curriculum to Include Soft Skill Training: Impacts on Health, Behaviour, Emotional Wellbeing and Occupational Aspirations." *Centre for Economic Performance Discussion Papers* 1360.

Lybbert, T. and Wydick, B. 2018. "Poverty, Aspirations, and the Economics of Hope." *Economic Development and Cultural Change* 66 (2).

Machia, L. and Oswald, A. 2021. "Physical Pain, Gender, and the State of the Economy in 146 Nations." *Social Science and Medicine* 287.

Mahler, A., Simmons, C., Frick, P. J., Steinberg, L., and Cauffman, E. 2017. "Aspirations, Expectations and Delinquency: The Moderating Effect of Impulse Control." *Journal of Youth and Adolescence* 46 (1): 1503–14.

Malecot, G. 1959. "Les Modeles Stochastiques Genetique de Population." Pub. Inst. Statist. Univ. of Paris, 8: 173–210.

Mann, M. 2004. "Self-Esteem in a Broad-Spectrum Approach for Mental Health Promotion." *Health Education Research* 19 (4): 357–72. https://doi.org/10.1093/her/cyg041.

Marziller, J. and Hall, J. 2009. "The Challenge of the Layard Initiative." *The Psychologist* 22: 396–99.

Mastrangelo, D. 2021. "Negative Emotions Hit Record High in 2020." *The Hill*, July 20.

McGrath, R. E., Brown, M., Westrich, B., and Han, H. 2021. "Representative Sampling of the VIA Assessment Suite for Adults." *Journal of Personality Assessment* 104 (3): 380–94. https://doi.org/10.1080/00223891.2021.1955692.

McIntosh, R., Ironson, G., and Kraus, N. 2021. "Keeping Hope Alive: Racial-Ethnic Disparities in Distress Tolerance Are Mediated by Religion/Spirituality Among African Americans." *Journal of Psychosomatic Research* 114.

Meadows Mental Health Policy Institute. 2020. "COVID-19 Briefing: Modeling the Effects of Collaborative Care and Medication-Assisted Treatment to Prevent COVID-Related Suicide and Overdose Deaths." https://mmhpi.org/wp-content/uploads/2020/09/COVID-MHSUDPrevention.pdf.

Medina, Richard et al. 2018. "The Geographies of Hate in America: A Regional Analysis." *Annals of American Association of Geographers* 108 (4).

Menninger, K. 1930. *The Human Mind.* New York: Alfred A. Knopf.

Montgomery, M. 2022. "The Gender Gap in Happiness." *Journal of Economic Behavior and Organization,* forthcoming.

Mullainathan, S. and Shafir, E. 2013. *Scarcity: The New Science of Having Less and How It Defines Our Lives.* New York: Henry Holt.

Nei, M. 1972. "Genetic Distance Between Populations." *American Naturalist* 106 (949): 283–92.

Nikolova, M. and Cnossen, F. 2022. "What Makes Work Meaningful and Why Economists Should Care about It." *Labour Economics,* forthcoming.

Nikolova, M., and Graham, C. 2022. "The Economics of Happiness." In *Handbook of Labor, Human Resources and Population Economics,* edited by K. F. Zimmerman. Cham, Switzerland: Springer International Publishing.

O'Connor, K. and Graham, C. 2019. "Longer, More Optimistic, Lives: Historic Optimism and Life Expectancy in the United States." *Journal of Economic Behavior and Organization* 168: 374–92.

Odermatt, R. and Stutzer, A. 2019. "(Mis-)Predicted Subjective Well-Being Following Life Events." *Journal of the European Economics Association* 17 (1).

O'Donnell, G. and Oswald, A. 2015. "National Well-Being Policy and a Weighted Approach to Human Feelings." *Ecological Economics* 120: 59–70.

OECD. 2016. *PISA 2015 Results (Volume I): Excellence and Equity in Education.* PISA, OCED Publishing. https://doi.org/10.1787/9789264266490-en.

Okamoto, K., Ohsuka, K., Shiraishi, T., Hukazawa, E., Wakasugi, S., and Furuta, K. 2002. "Comparability of Epidemiological Information between Self- and Interviewer-Administered Questionnaires." *Journal of Clinical Epidemiology* 55 (5): 505–11. https://doi.org/10.1016/S0895-4356(01)00515-7.

Ong, A., Bergeman, A. S., Bisconti, T., and Wallace, K. 2006. "Psychological Resilience, Positive Emotions, and Successful Adaptation to Stress in Later Life." *Journal of Perspectives on Psychological Science* 91 (4): 730–49.

Pew Charitable Trusts. 2017. *How Income Volatility Interacts with American Families' Financial Security: An Examination of Gains, Losses, and Household Economic Experiences."* Report.

Piazza, J. 2015. "The Determinants of Right-Wing Terrorism in the U.S.A.: Economic Grievance, Societal Change and Political Resentment." *Conflict Management and Peace Science* 34 (1): 52–80.

Pinto, S., Bencsik, P., Chuluun, C., and Graham, C. 2020. "Presidential Elections, Divided Politics, and Happiness in the U.S.A." *Economica* 88 (349): 189–207.

Piper, A. 2022. "Optimism, Pessimism and Life Satisfaction: An Empirical Investigation." *International Review of Economics* 69: 177–208. https://doi.org/10.1007/s12232-022-00390-8.

Pleeging, E., Burger, M., and Van Exel, J. 2021. "The Relations between Hope and Subjective Well-Being: A Literature Overview and Empirical Analysis." *Applied Research on Quality of Life Studies* 16: 1019–1041.

Powell-Jackson, T., Pereira, S. K., Dutt, V., Tougher, S., Haldar, K., and Kumar, P. 2016. "Cash Transfers, Maternal Depression and Emotional Well-Being: Quasi-Experimental Evidence from India's Janani Suraksha Yojana Program." *Social Science & Medicine* 162: 210–18.

Proto, E. and Oswald, A. 2016. "National Happiness and Genetic Distance: A Cautious Exploration." *Economic Journal* 127: 2127–2152.

Putnam, R. 2015. *Our Kids: The American Dream in Crisis.* New York: Simon and Schuster.

Quinones, S. 2015. *Dreamlands: The True Tale of America's Opiate Epidemic.* New York: Bloomsbury.

Ramchad, R., Gordon, J., and Pearson, J. 2021. "Trends in Suicide by Race and Ethnicity in the United States." *JAMA Network Open 4* (5). https://jamanetwork.com/journals/jamanetworkopen/fullarticle/2780380.

Rauch, J. 2021. *The Constitution of Knowledge: A Defense of the Truth.* Washington, DC: The Brookings Institution Press.

Ray, D. 2006. "Aspirations, Poverty, and Economic Change." In *Understanding Poverty*, edited by A. Banerjee, D. Mookherjee, and R. Benabou. Oxford: Oxford University Press.

———. 2016. "Aspirations and the Development Treadmill." *Journal of Human Development and Capabilities* 17 (3): 309–23. https://doi.org/10.1080/19452829.2016.1211597.

Reeves, R. 2018. *Dream Hoarders.* Washington, DC: Brookings Institution Press.

Robert Wood Johnson Foundation. 2014. *Commission to Build a Healthier America.* Princeton: RWJF.

Ross, P. H. 2019. "Occupation Aspirations, Education Investment, and Cognitive Outcomes: Evidence from Indian Adolescents." *World Development* 123. https://doi.org/10.1016/j.worlddev.2019.104613.

Ruiz Pozuelo, J., Desborough, L., Stein, A., and Cipriani, A. 2021. "Systematic Review and Meta-Analysis: Depressive Symptoms and Risky Behaviours among Adolescents in Low- and Middle-Income Countries." *Journal of the American Academy of Child and Adolescent Psychiatry* 61 (2): 255–76. https://doi.org/10.1016/j.jaac.2021.05.005.

Ryon, H. S. and Gleason, M. 2014. "The Role of Locus of Control in Daily Life." *Personality and Social Psychology Bulletin* 40 (1): 121–31.

Safford, V. 2004. "The Gates of Hope." *The Nation*, September 20.

Sawhill, I. 2019. *The Forgotten Americans.* New Haven, CT: Yale University Press.

Sawyer, S. M., Afifi, R. A., Bearinger, L. H., Blakemore, S. J., Dick, B., Ezeh, A. C., and Patton, G. C. 2012. "Adolescence: A Foundation for Future Health." *The Lancet* 379 (9826): 1630–1640. https://doi.org/10.1016/S0140-6736(12)60072-5.

Schmid, K. L., Phelps, E., and Lerner, R. M. 2011. "Constructing Positive Futures: Modeling the Relationship between Adolescents' Hopeful Future Expectations and Intentional Self-Regulation in Predicting Positive Youth Development. *Journal of Adolescence* 34 (6): 1127–1135. https://doi.org/10.1016/j.adolescence.2011.07.009.

Schrank, B., Hayward, M., Stanghelli, G., and Davidson, L. 2011. "Hope in Psychiatry." *Advances in Psychiatric Treatment* 17 (3): 227–35.

Schrank, B., Stanghellini, G., and Slade, M. 2008. "Hope in Psychiatry: A Review of the Literature." *Acta Psychiatrica Scandinavica* 118 (6): 421–33.

Schwandt, H. 2016. "Unmet Aspirations as an Explanation for the U-Curve." *Journal of Economic Behavior and Organization* 122: 71–87.

Schwarzer, R. and Jerusalem, M. 1995. "Generalized Self-Efficacy Scale." In *Measures in Health Psychology: A User's Portfolio. Causal and Control Beliefs*, edited by J. Weinman, S. Wright, and M. Johnston, 35–37. Windsor, U.K.: NFER-NELSON.

Sebastian, C., Burnett, S., and Blakemore, S. J. 2008. "Development of the Self-Concept during Adolescence." *Trends in Cognitive Sciences* 12 (11): 441–46. https://doi.org/10.1016/j.tics.2008.07.008.

Sipsma, H. L., Ickovics, J. R., Lin, H., and Kershaw, T. S. 2013. "The Impact of Future Expectations on Adolescent Sexual Risk Behavior." *Journal of Youth and Adolescence* 44 (1): 170–83. https://doi.org/10.1007/s10964-013-0082-7.

Snyder, C. R. 2000. *The Handbook of Hope: Theory, Measures, and Applications*. North Holland, Amsterdam: Elsevier Science and Technology.

Steinberg, L. 2004. "Risk Taking in Adolescence: What Changes, and Why?" *Annals of the New York Academy of Science* 1021 (1): 51–58. https://doi.org/10.1196/annals.1308.005.

Steptoe, A. and Wardle, J. 2001. "Locus of Control and Health Behaviour Revisited: a Multivariate Analysis of Young Adults from 18 Countries." *British Journal of Psychology* 92 (4): 659–72.

Stone, A. A. and Mackie, C., eds. 2013. *Subjective Well-Being: Measuring Happiness, Suffering, and Other Dimensions of Experience*. Washington DC: National Academies Press.

UNESCO. 2018. *Accountability in Education: Meeting Our Commitments*. New York: UNESCO Global Education Report Series.

Unützer, J., Harbin, H., Schoenbaum, M., and Druss, B. 2013. *The Collaborative Care Model: An Approach for Integrating Physical and Mental Health Care in Medicaid Health Homes*. Health Home Information Resource Center.

Vance, J. D. 2016. *Hillbilly Elegy: A Memoir of a Family and Culture in Crisis*. New York: Harper Collins.

Weiss, A., King, J. E., Inoue-Murayama, M., Matsuzawa, T., and Oswald, A. 2012. "Evidence for a Midlife Crisis in Great Apes Consistent with the U-Shape in Human Well-Being." *Proceedings of the National Academy of Sciences* 109 (49): 19949–19952.

Woolridge, J. M. 2010. *Econometric Analysis of Cross Section and Panel Data*. Cambridge, MA: MIT Press.

Yamada, G. 2006. "Retornos a la Educación Superior en el Mercado Laboral: ¿Vale la Pena el Esfuerzo?" Centro de Investigación, Universidad Del Pacífico in Lima, Peru. Working Papers 06–13.

Young, H. P. 1998. *Individual Strategy and Social Structures: An Evolutionary Theory of Institutions*. Princeton, NJ: Princeton University Press.

Young, S. G. and McGrath, R. E. 2020. "Character Strengths as Predictors of Trust and Cooperation in Economic Decision-Making." *Journal of Trust Research* 10 (2): 159–79. https://doi.org/10.1080/21515581.2021.1922911.

Youngblood, M. 2020. "Extremist Ideology as Complex Contagion: The Spread of Far-Right Radicalization in the United States between 2005–2017." *Humanities and Social Sciences Communications* 7 (49).

INDEX

Page numbers followed by *f* or *t* refer to a figure or table.

labor markets: impact of COVID-19 pandemic on, 18; importance of restoring hopes for, 123–24; inadequate education for, 4, 5, 33, 8; labor force dropout rates, 14; links with despair, 3, 12, 43, 47, 117; mental health and, 102; OLF population, 12, 43–44; preparation of adolescents for, 52–53, 58, 101–2, 106–7, 113–14; private-public partnerships, 117–205

Latin America: comparative optimism levels of, 7; resilience of poor people in, xii; rich versus poor gaps in, 11

Layard, Richard, 112

Levelling Up initiative (U.K.), xi

Levenson, Hanna, 60

life satisfaction: age and, 28–29; comparison to optimism/pessimism, 26; components of, 61; determinants of, 21–22; differences across races, cultures, populations, 28–29; health outcomes and, 25; hedonic well-being and, 22–23; impact of, 22; income inequality and, 34; Peru survey findings, 70–71; in the United Kingdom, 109, 111; well-being metrics of, 105–6; of women versus men, 132n4

Lima, Peru. *See* Peru, study of aspirations and personality traits

locus of control, 26, 28, 32, 56, 60–61, 70, 71*t*, 74*t*, 77, 82

loneliness: comparison to solitude, 111; definition/features of, 111–12, 114; of elderly adults in the U.K., 113; importance of addressing, 102, 104; of respondents in Missouri study, 89; strategies for reducing, 108, 111; study of COVID-19 and, 112; What Works Centre for Wellbeing study findings on, 111

Lopez, T., 40

low-income whites: deaths of despair data for, 12; decline in education and health of, 35–36, 80; declining income levels of, 80; and declin-

ing levels of hope, 29, 35–37, 80; declining marriage rates of, 92; despair of, 2, 3, 85; disintegration of marriages among, 37; low educational aspirations of, 85; and optimism, 6–7, 13, 56; response patterns in Thinking about the Future Survey, 83–85; stress and worry levels of, 29; supportive programs for, 132; types of decline of, 35

Lybbert, Travis, 26

Malecot, 39–40

marriage: declining rates for low-income whites, 36–37, 92; increasing rates for wealthy couples, 92; optimism, life satisfaction, and, 26

Maryland Behavioral Health Administration, 116

May, Theresa, 113

McCoy, Art, 81

McGrath, Robert, 38, 41

McIntosh, Roger, 38

Meadows Mental Health Policy Institute, 115

Menninger, Karl, 3

mental health: benefits of private-public partnerships for, 117–20; impact of COVID-19 pandemic on, 12, 96; impact of drug addiction on, 4; impact of loneliness on, 111–12; importance of hope for, 3, 25; increasing access to care, in the U.K., 114–15; influence of 5-HTTLPR gene on, 7; influence of unemployment on, 45; limited rural access to care, 103; of low-income African Americans, 13; need for community focus on, 99–100; need for early diagnosis and treatment of, 132; new forms of support for, 114–17; for poor less-than-college-educated whites, 14; primary care-based approaches to, 115; psychological distress and, 26, 38, 65, 101;